9F3B6681

FROM SCRATCH

Dedication

To my parents, for always letting me mess up
your lovely kitchen to bake in.

And to my audience, for always having
my back and giving me my dream job.
This book is for all of you.

ALICE KELLY

FROM SCRATCH

80 FOOLPROOF RECIPES BY @FROMSCRATCHBAKER,
FROM EASY TRAYBAKES TO SHOWSTOPPING CAKES

NINE BEAN ROWS

Contents

Breakfast bakes

Cookies & biscuits

Traybakes & bars

Cakes, cupcakes & muffins

Tarts, pastry & sweet breads

Other sweet things

Introduction

Growing up, I was encouraged to take any path I wanted in life and trusted – especially in the kitchen. I have been baking since I was three years old (with supervision, of course). At age seven, I kicked my mum out of the kitchen and told my grandad to inform her that I was more than capable of baking on my own (sorry, Mum!). That confidence in the kitchen stuck with me.

My entire childhood was spent experimenting with different flavours and types of cakes. In all honesty, I never baked cakes to eat them – the process was what enthralled me. If you had asked me at three years old and today, at 22 years old, what my dream job is, I would have always said it's a baker.

But it's not all been sweet. Things took a turn in my final few years of secondary school, when my mental health deteriorated quickly and I eventually stopped attending school altogether. I lost passion for everything and I barely left the house. Life felt frightening in ways I couldn't explain, and fear became my only feeling. I remember crying so hard before one exam that my hands seized up and I couldn't move them for hours. In that moment, I knew I couldn't live a life where I was afraid of everything outside my house. Something had to change.

During the pandemic I would take my daily stroll through the local village and pass a coffee trailer operating out of a horse-box. I kept that cool business idea in the back of my mind for my future, but a couple months later, just before my 18th birthday, I was scrolling on a second-hand website when I stumbled across a vintage (and very dilapidated) horse-box. To me, it was gold. My dad drove me an hour to pick it up. It was filthy, falling apart and completely unfit for food service, but €590 later, it was mine! I finally felt like I had a bit of purpose. This is what I wanted to do.

I scraped through my final exams (barely, I might add) and poured everything into renovating that horse-box. At this point I was sending video updates on the construction of the box to my friends and they convinced me to post one on TikTok. I fell asleep after posting the first video and woke up the next morning to 100,000 followers and 15 million views. I was flabbergasted! For five months straight, I worked on it almost every day to bring it back to life. I fitted a service window, new floorboards, insulation, built a whole new back door ... I could go on. Everything in that horse-box was built from scratch, which is why I chose the name @fromscratchbaker.

Around the time I finished the horse-box, university offers were released and I was accepted into a culinary arts course. On the very first day, the old familiar feeling returned. Walking into that building made me feel physically ill, not because of the university itself, but because I already knew deep down that it wasn't right for me. I dropped out after two months. Once again, I felt like a failure. All I wanted to do was retreat to my bedroom and disappear again.

Right as I dropped out, I got an email that gave me a glimmer of hope. I was offered the incredible opportunity to open my horse-box bakery in the heart of Dublin, next to the famous Molly Malone statue. I worked from early in the morning to very late in the evening for three days straight. I was exhausted afterwards, but those three days were a huge turning point in my life. I decided to apply to bakery school the following year.

To afford to open the horse-box bakery more often, I needed a job. I didn't feel particularly stable, but I applied for a waitressing job anyway. That job turned out to be one of the best decisions I ever made. Hospitality taught me how to pour a proper pint of Guinness and introduced me to other people's stories (some good, some bad) instead of worrying about my own all the time. My biggest concern in that job was getting everyone's toasted sandwiches out on time.

But several months into the job, everything shifted again. After work one evening, I hopped into my mum's car, brushed my knuckles across my chest while putting on my seatbelt and felt a lump. I knew instantly that something was wrong. I had a GP appointment the next day for something unrelated and asked the doctor to check it, hoping I was just imagining the lump. I was definitely not imagining it. I was referred to a breast surgeon and had the lump biopsied. Reading the word 'benign' is a feeling I'll never forget – the relief was incredible. But due to its size, the tumour still had to be removed.

I had a lumpectomy that July and apparently woke up speaking Tagalog to the nurses (I've no idea where that came from!). Recovery was hard. I wasn't allowed to lift anything heavy, which knocked me back more than I realised. I couldn't bake for months. In my final days of working as a waitress, when I was mostly making pots of tea and feeling quite useless, I found out I'd been accepted into bakery school. I stayed in the toilet cubicle I was in, reading that email over and over. I knew this was my final shot at university.

I reluctantly left my waitressing job to focus on a few upcoming events for the horse-box bakery and threw myself into a new chapter of life. I met people who had followed my journey online and I slowly began to feel like myself again. For the first time in months, the brain fog lifted and I didn't need to distract myself with work.

Then I found another lump. The tumour had returned. I genuinely thought I wasn't going to be able to attend bakery school and my life would be in shambles all over again. Thankfully, the tumour was smaller and still benign, so for now, it stays with me. I even named it Simon so I can give out to him.

A little while later, I started bakery school. From day one, I knew this was where I'd been meant to be all along. I loved every second of it (except for the accounting classes!). After my struggles in secondary school, it felt surreal to enjoy education and I made some lifelong friends along the way too.

I got my driver's licence and I travelled to see family in the UK for the first time in years. I went from not leaving the house for months to building a full life for myself, including social media being my full-time job (writing that still feels a bit surreal!). I usually just say I'm a baker when most people ask me what my job is, because trying to explain that I make videos of baking things like frog doughnuts can be a bit hard to explain sometimes! But with more than 1 million followers on YouTube and millions of followers across my other platforms, I'm still speechless when you guys say hi in the street.

Which brings us up to recent times. While writing this book, I faced a few more setbacks. I was diagnosed with haemochromatosis, which meant I spent many weekends writing with sore arms from blood-letting sessions. I was also diagnosed with PoTS, a condition whose name still makes me giggle, given how many pots and pans I own, though the reality is much less funny. Thankfully, I manage both of those conditions now. It's hard to keep me from baking!

By the age of 22, I've already lived several different lives, and I wouldn't change a single one. From baking at three years old with my mum to getting into bakery school and hitting 1 million YouTube subscribers, every version of me has led here, to writing my debut book.

These recipes have carried me through the best and worst moments of my life. My parents' kitchen has been witness to burnt caramel, collapsed sponge cakes, bread as flat as a tortilla and some questionable croissants that could have been used as doorstops. It has also seen the joy and love I put into every recipe in this book. Throughout it all, baking has been my constant. I've found that there are few things the magical combination of butter, sugar and flour can't make better.

Whether you're a first-time baker or a confident measure-the-vanilla-with-your-heart type of person, this book is for you. I've included simple bakes all the way up to making your own rough puff pastry, with lots in between. There's something here for every type of baker and every kind of mood, whether you want to whip up something sweet quickly and easily or challenge yourself to learn a new technique. No matter what you make, I hope baking brings you as much comfort and happiness as it's brought me.

Why I weigh all my ingredients (even liquids)

Baking is chemistry, not guesswork. Weighing your ingredients gives you the most control and therefore the best chance at getting the recipe right.

A gram is always a gram. A cup, however, depends on how tightly an ingredient is packed, what cup you're using and what ingredient is being measured. One person's cup of flour can easily be 20 grams heavier or lighter than another's, and in baking, that matters! That's why in bakeries and culinary schools, ingredients are weighed, not scooped. I also find it incredibly convenient being able to measure all my ingredients into one bowl on a scale rather than dirtying several cups.

Having said all that, I have still included cup measurements for those who haven't converted to weighing your ingredients (yet!). I promise your baked goods will taste delicious no matter what measurements you use from this book!

line a round tin

1. Lightly grease the base and inside wall of the tin with butter, oil or baking spray. This helps the cake to release from the tin and the grease sticks the non-stick baking paper to the tin so it doesn't slide around.

2. Put the tin on a piece of non-stick baking paper that is larger than the base of the tin. Using a pencil, draw around the base of the tin.

3. Cut out this circle and put it in the base of the greased tin, with the pencil marks facing down so they don't transfer to the cake.

4. Cut a long strip of paper that's the same height as the side of the tin. Gently press this strip onto the greased sides of the tin, overlapping it slightly where the two ends meet.

5. Run your fingers around the tin to make sure the paper is flush against the sides and the base, otherwise any wrinkles will show up in the baked cake.

line a rectangular tin

1. Lightly grease the base and inside walls of the tin with butter, oil or baking spray. This helps the cake to release from the tin and the grease sticks the non-stick baking paper to the tin so it doesn't slide around.

2. Cut a piece of non-stick baking paper that's long enough to cover the base and two opposite sides of the tin. Put it in the tin, leaving an overhang on each side to lift the cake out after it's baked.

3. Cut another strip of paper to fit the remaining two sides, also with an overhang. Put it in the tin perpendicular to the first strip so the base is fully covered and all four sides are lined.

4. Run your fingers around the tin to make sure the paper is flush against the sides and the base, otherwise any wrinkles will show up in the baked cake.

soften butter

When a recipe calls for softened butter, it means butter that's at room temperature, not fridge cold. The butter should be soft enough to press with your finger, not melted. Why is this important? Because if the butter is too cold, it won't dissolve into the sugar when you cream them together; if it's too warm, it won't hold any air.

There are two easy ways to soften butter: the countertop method if you've planned ahead or the warm bowl method if you've forgotten to let your butter soften before you started baking (we've all been there!).

The countertop method

1. Take the butter out of the fridge and leave it on the work surface for around 30 minutes, depending on the temperature of your kitchen (longer in the wintertime, maybe less time in the summer).
2. It's ready when you can press it easily with your finger.

The warm bowl method

1. Put the butter on a plate.
2. Fill a heatproof bowl (like a Pyrex bowl) with hot water and let it sit for 1 minute. (Don't use a glass bowl that's not heatproof, as they have a tendency to shatter!)
3. After a minute, empty the water from the bowl and dry it. Put the warm bowl upside down over the butter.
4. Leave for 5–10 minutes, until the butter is soft. It's ready when you can press it easily with your finger.

cream butter and sugar

Creaming butter and sugar is one of the most important foundational techniques in baking. When done properly, it dissolves the sugar into the butter, creating tiny air bubbles in the mixture, which makes your cakes light and fluffy.

1. Put the soft, room-temperature butter and sugar in a mixing bowl. Use a handheld electric mixer or a stand mixer. Don't cream butter and sugar by hand unless you want a workout!

2. Beat the mixture on high speed until it becomes a lot paler in colour and visibly fluffier. This can take several minutes. Stop occasionally to scrape down the sides of the bowl to make sure everything gets evenly combined. Speaking from experience, you don't want any butter clumps in your cake batter.

3. After 3–5 minutes, check the mixture: stop the mixer, then using your fingertips, take a small pinch of the mixture and rub it between your fingers. If you feel any sugar particles, it's not ready yet, so keep beating and check it again after another minute or two. When you can't feel any sugar particles and the mixture is light and fluffy throughout, you can move on to the next step in the recipe.

rub butter into flour

Rubbing butter into flour creates a tender crumb in pastry by coating the flour with fat, thereby limiting its gluten development and giving the pastry a short, crumbly finish. Once you get a feel for it, it's incredibly satisfying to do!

1. Start with very cold butter. Cut the butter into small cubes, as they are easier to rub into the flour than large pieces.

2. Put the butter cubes in the bowl of flour and toss them around gently so the cubes are fully coated in flour. This stops the pieces of butter from clumping together.

3. Using only your fingertips (not your palms, as they are warmer and will melt the butter), lift small amounts of the flour and butter while gently rubbing them together. Let it fall back into the bowl as you work through all the butter cubes.

4. Work quickly, as the goal is to flatten the butter into the flour without warming it up. If you need to stop, put the bowl in the fridge to prevent the butter from melting.

5. Continue rubbing the butter into the flour until the mixture looks like fine breadcrumbs. You'll know it's ready when you grab a handful of the mixture and press it together firmly in your hand, and it stays in that shape. There will also be no visible chunks of butter. (Though depending on the recipe, like for rough puff pastry, a slightly coarser breadcrumb texture and larger butter chunks may be preferred.) You could also do this in a food processor by quickly blitzing the butter and flour together, but rubbing it in by hand gives you the most control.

make a buttermilk substitute

Did you know what you can make a buttermilk substitute using regular whole milk and vinegar or lemon juice? This is a handy trick if you don't have any buttermilk or if a recipe calls for only a small amount, like in my chocolate fudge cake on page 124.

1. Measure however much buttermilk you need using whole milk instead.

2. Add 1 tablespoon of white wine vinegar, apple cider vinegar or lemon juice. Stir for a few seconds, then set aside for 5–10 minutes, until the milk curdles and thickens.

sift dry ingredients

Sifting helps remove any lumps from dry ingredients and evenly combines them. It also adds air to the dry ingredients, which acts as a raising agent. While it can feel like an unnecessary step and the temptation to chuck the flour in unsifted is understandable, do take the extra time to sift. No one wants a cake with clumps of flour in it or icing with lumps of dry icing sugar.

1. Always weigh or measure your ingredients before sifting. Sifting incorporates air into the dry ingredients, so the weight or cup measurement after sifting will be less accurate.

2. Use a fine mesh sieve. Hold the sieve a few centimetres above your mixing bowl to allow air to pass through the dry ingredients as they fall. Be careful not to dip the bottom of the sieve into any wet ingredients, as it will no longer let dry ingredients pass through and will become a sticky mess that you don't want to have to clean, believe me!

3. Tap or shake the sieve lightly until the dry ingredients pass through. If small lumps remain in the base of the sieve, gently press them through with the back of a clean spoon.

4. If any hard lumps refuse to pass through, they should be discarded.

fold dry ingredients into wet

Folding is a gentle mixing method used to combine dry ingredients into a wet mixture without knocking out the air you've worked so hard to incorporate. It's an important technique to give light cakes the perfect texture.

1. Sprinkle the dry ingredients all over the wet mixture – don't dump them all in one place. This makes the folding more even across the mixture and prevents any deflation.

2. Dip a spatula down to the base of the bowl in the centre.

3. Sweep the spatula along the bottom of the bowl, then up the side and gently lift the mixture over itself.

4. Give the bowl a quarter-turn and repeat.

5. Keep going until the mixture is just combined. Stop folding as soon as you no longer see any streaks of dry ingredients. Overmixing will deflate the mixture and undo all your careful folding.

knead dough

Kneading dough develops the gluten in the flour, which gives dough good structure, elasticity and strength for rising. Though I use a stand mixer for most of my kneading, learning how to do it by hand is a good skill to have.

1. Lightly sprinkle your work surface with flour. Turn the dough out of the bowl onto the floured surface and shape it into a rough ball.

2. Using the heel of your hand, push the dough away from you while stretching it slightly.

3. Fold the stretched dough back over itself towards your body.

4. Give the dough a quarter-turn and repeat the push, fold, turn motion.

5. Keeping a steady rhythm, knead the dough until the surface of the ball becomes smooth and springy when poked. Take a small cutting from the centre of the dough and stretch it between your fingertips. If it spreads thinly and creates a 'window' without breaking that is thin enough for you to see through, then the dough is ready.

blind bake pastry

Blind baking is the process of partially or fully baking a pastry case before adding a wet or no-bake filling. It prevents the dreaded soggy bottom and keeps the pastry crisp.

1. Roll out your pastry and carefully line the tin with it, pressing it gently into the corners and ridges. Trim the edges.

2. Lightly prick the base of the pastry all over with a fork. This helps steam escape and reduces the risk of the pastry puffing up.

3. Scrunch up a sheet of non-stick baking paper, then smooth it back out and put it on top of the pastry case. Fill the paper with an oven-safe weight (I use ceramic baking beans or dried rice), making sure these weights reach the sides and cover the base completely.

4. Bake the lined and weighted pastry case in the preheated oven for the specified time in the recipe.

5. Remove the baking beans by lifting out the filled paper and setting it aside to allow the weights to cool. Baking beans can get very hot, so don't touch them and don't put them back in a plastic tub right away. (I'm speaking from experience here – you don't want to clean up melted plastic!)

6. Bake the pastry case again, uncovered, if the recipe calls for it. Otherwise, set it aside on a wire rack until you're ready to fill it.

whisk egg whites to stiff peaks

Whisking egg whites to stiff peaks is all about incorporating air into your baked goods. It's an essential technique for making meringues, mousses and light sponges.

1. Start by scalding your heatproof mixing bowl with hot water. This will get rid of any trace of grease, which prevents egg whites from whisking properly. Make sure your bowl and whisk are completely dry before beginning.

2. Separate the egg whites from the yolks, ensuring no yolk gets into the whites. Egg yolk contains fat and will prevent the egg whites from whisking to a peak. To be extra safe, separate each egg into a small bowl before adding the whites to the larger bowl. That way, if any yolk gets into the whites, the entire batch won't be ruined.

3. Using a handheld whisk or a stand mixer fitted with the whisk attachment, start beating on a low to medium speed until the egg whites become foamy and opaque. Adding a pinch of salt or cream of tartar helps the egg whites to whisk.

4. Once the whites are foamy, increase the speed and keep whisking until the egg whites start to hold their shape.

5. At this stage, soft peaks will form but gently fall over when the whisk is lifted. Keep going!

6. Continue whisking until the peaks stand straight up when the whisk is lifted and the mixture is smooth and glossy. This is called stiff peaks and is now ready to use.

whip cream

Whipping cream incorporates air into liquid cream, transforming it into something stable and spoonable. Timing really matters here. Too little whipping and the cream won't hold its shape; too much and you'll end up with curdled cream (or even butter if you really overdo it!).

1. Use cream directly from the fridge and pour it into a cold bowl. (I refrigerate my bowl and whisk too.)

2. Start on a low to medium speed to prevent the cream from splashing everywhere. It will start to become frothy before it begins to stiffen.

3. Increase the speed after 1 minute. Watch the cream begin to thicken and the whisk leave its shape in the cream.

4. Stop mixing to see how thick the cream is. If it pours off the whisk, it's not ready yet. When the cream holds its shape when held upright on the whisk and is smooth, it's ready. Be warned, though, that your cream can go from not ready to overwhipped in a matter of seconds, so stop and check it often if you think it's getting close.

5. If you whip your cream a little too much and it has become slightly grainy, pouring in a little liquid cream and stirring it through helps bring it back to the soft, smooth texture you want.

6. Put the whipped cream in the fridge if you aren't using it right away.

BREAKFAST BAKES

Irish soda bread

500g (4¼ cups) plain flour, plus extra for dusting

200g (1⅔ cups) strong white flour

70g (⅓ cup) salted butter, cold and cubed

10g (2 tsp) baking soda

a pinch of salt

400g (1⅔ cups) buttermilk

100g (⅔ cup) raisins (optional)

I make this for my dad, who loves raisins in his soda bread. Though less traditional than a plain soda, I enjoy the sweet pops the raisins give to an otherwise quite heavy bread. As a variation, roll the dough into a rectangle and stamp it out into circles to make soda scones. Brush them with egg wash, then bake them in the oven for 14–16 minutes.

Prep: Preheat the oven to 180°C (350°F). Line a baking tray with non-stick baking paper, then lightly sprinkle the paper with plain flour.

Make the bread: Put the two flours, butter, baking soda and a pinch of salt in a large bowl and whisk to combine. (Don't add too much baking soda or your bread will turn green – trust me on this one!) Using your fingers, crumble the butter into the flour mixture until a breadcrumb texture forms.

Make a well in the flour mixture and pour in half of the buttermilk. Using one hand held like a claw and keeping your other hand clean, mix until a shaggy dough forms. Pour in the rest of the buttermilk and add the raisins (if using). Bring the dough together into a ball.

Lightly dust a clean work surface with a little plain flour. Tip the dough out onto the work surface, then knead the dough for just 1 minute, until the surface is smooth and the shape is a uniform ball. Sprinkle the surface of the dough generously with plain flour and smooth it over the top with your hands.

Put the dough on your lined, floured tray. Using a sharp knife, cut it down the centre and then again horizontally. The cuts should form a cross that divides the dough into quarters. In Irish folklore this was done to let the fairies out so they wouldn't curse the bread, but really it's to make sure the bread rises evenly.

Bake: Bake in the preheated oven for 30–35 minutes, until golden brown. It can be hard to tell if soda bread is baked fully due to the flour coating on top, so the best way to check is to flip the bread over to make sure the base has a nice golden crust.

Serve: Leave to cool on the tray, then cut into slices to serve.

Store: Covered at room temperature for up to four days. It will dry out a little, but it makes excellent toast. If you're worried about it crumbling or breaking up in the toaster, melt a knob of butter in a frying pan on a medium-high heat and fry it for 2–3 minutes on each side instead.

Banana bread

Makes 1 loaf

110g (½ cup) salted butter, softened

150g (¾ cup) caster sugar

50g (¼ cup) vegetable oil

2 medium eggs

1 tsp vanilla bean paste

2 large, over-ripe bananas – the browner, the better!

300g (2½ cups) self-raising flour

½ tsp ground cinnamon

½ tsp ground nutmeg

Optional add-ins:

a handful of chocolate chips, dried cranberries, or chopped walnuts or pecans

Ah, banana bread. This is still one of my most-requested, most popular recipes.

Prep: Preheat the oven to 180°C (350°F). Line a 900g (2lb) loaf tin with non-stick baking paper.

Make the bread: Using an electric mixer, beat the butter and sugar in a large mixing bowl for a few minutes, until pale and fluffy.

Add the oil, eggs and vanilla and beat until combined.

Put the bananas in a separate bowl and mash them until there are no large chunks. Add the mashed bananas to the butter and sugar mixture and mix until well combined.

Sift in the flour, cinnamon and nutmeg. Fold through until there is no visible flour in the batter. Stir in the chocolate chips, dried cranberries or nuts (if using).

Scrape the batter into the lined loaf tin, making sure to spread it evenly into the corners.

Bake: Bake in the preheated oven for 55–60 minutes, until the loaf is deep brown on top and a skewer inserted into the middle comes out clean and dry.

Serve: Let the banana bread cool in the tin before removing. Cut into thick slices to serve.

Store: In an airtight container at room temperature for up to five days.

Apple cinnamon rolls

For the dough:

700g (5¾ cups) strong white flour, plus extra for dusting

100g (½ cup) caster sugar

1 x 7g sachet (2¼ tsp) of fast-action dried yeast

2 medium eggs

300g (1¼ cups) cool water

1 tsp vanilla bean paste

150g (⅔ cup) salted butter, cut into 15g (1 tbsp) pieces

For the filling:

30g (2 tbsp) salted butter, melted

100g (½ cup) caster sugar

3 tbsp ground cinnamon

2 large cooking apples (such as Bramley), peeled, cored and diced into small cubes

For the drizzle:

200g (1⅔ cups) icing sugar

2 tsp lemon juice

a splash of cool water

Cinnamon rolls are great, but adding chunks of soft, sweet apple makes them so much better.

Make the dough: Put the flour, sugar, yeast, eggs, cool water and vanilla in the bowl of a stand mixer fitted with the dough hook. Knead on a high speed for 3 minutes, until it comes together into a dough. (This dough is best made in a stand mixer, but you can make it by hand if you want.)

After the 3 minutes are up, start adding the butter one piece at a time, waiting until it has been thoroughly incorporated until you add the next piece. Once all the butter has been added, turn the speed down to medium-low and keep mixing for another 10 minutes, until the dough is smooth, shiny and elastic.

Wrap the top of the bowl with cling film and leave it in a warm, draught-free place until it has doubled in size. This typically takes 2 hours, but it depends on how warm it is.

Add the filling: After the dough has doubled in size, line a deep 24cm x 35.5cm (9½in x 14in) baking tin with non-stick baking paper. Lightly dust a clean work surface with a little flour, then tip the dough out and roll it into a 30cm x 50cm (12in x 20in) rectangle. Dough can be tricky and sometimes it won't want to stretch when you try to roll it. To prevent tears, leave it alone and let it rest for a few minutes before rolling it out again.

Using a pastry brush, spread the melted butter over the entire rectangle of dough. Put the sugar and cinnamon in a small bowl and mix together, then sprinkle it all over the dough. Scatter over the diced apples.

Starting with the long edge that's furthest away from you, roll the dough tightly into a cylinder towards your body. Rolling towards you gives you more control, plus you can see if any filling squishes out.

Using a sharp knife, cut the dough into 12 even slices. Put the slices in the lined tin, spirals facing up.

Cover the tin with cling film. Leave in a warm place for 1 hour to let the rolls rise slightly.

Bake: When the hour is nearly up, preheat the oven to 180°C (350°F).

Bake the rolls in the middle of the preheated oven for 30–35 minutes, until they are nicely puffed up and golden on top.

Let the rolls cool in the tin for several minutes before inverting the tin and flipping them out to continue cooling on a wire rack.

For the drizzle: In a small bowl, combine the icing sugar and lemon juice with just enough cool water to make a paste. Spread or drizzle this over the rolls to add extra sweetness.

Store: In an airtight container in the fridge for up to three days. Put them in the microwave for 20 seconds to reheat.

Apple turnovers

Makes 12

For the rough puff pastry:

300g (2½ cups) plain flour, plus extra for dusting

175g (¾ cup) salted butter, cold and cubed

1 tbsp ground cinnamon

50g (¼ cup) cool water

30g (2 tbsp) salted butter, softened

For the filling:

1 large cooking apple (such as Bramley), peeled, cored and diced into tiny chunks

30g (1½ tbsp) caster sugar

For the egg wash:

1 medium egg

A classic apple turnover is one of my go-tos in a bakery. It's hard to beat when it's served while still slightly warm with a big scoop of vanilla ice cream. This recipe uses homemade rough puff pastry, which is easier to make than you might think – do try it! Or you can use two sheets of ready-rolled shop-bought puff pastry instead.

Make the rough puff pastry: Put the flour, 175g (¾ cup) cold butter and cinnamon in a medium bowl. Putting the cinnamon in the pastry rather than the filling is less overpowering and it also keeps the apple a lovely bright green colour. Using your fingertips, rub the butter into the flour, but leave large chunks of butter that aren't fully incorporated.

Pour in the cool water and bring everything together into a ball. If it's too dry, add a little more water, 1 teaspoon at a time, just until it comes together.

Lightly dust your clean work surface with a little flour. Tip out the dough, then roll it into a small square. Wrap in cling film and pop it in the freezer for 20 minutes.

When you take the dough out of the freezer, lightly dust your work surface with a little flour again. Unwrap the dough, then roll it out into a 20cm x 25cm (8in x 10in) rectangle.

Spread half of the softened butter over the surface of the dough, then cut it in half. Put one half on top of the other half, with the buttered sides pressed together. Wrap in cling film and freeze for another 20 minutes.

Roll the dough out on the lightly floured work surface into a 20cm x 25cm (8in x 10in) rectangle again. Spread the rest of the softened butter over the surface of the rolled dough and cut it in half again. Once again, put one half on top of the other half, with the buttered sides pressed together. Wrap in cling film and freeze for 20 minutes while you make the filling.

Make the filling: Pour a splash of water into a large saucepan – just enough to cover the base – then add the apple pieces and put the pan on a high heat. Bring to a boil, then reduce the heat and cook until the apple chunks are fork tender. Remove the pan from the heat and drain any excess liquid from the pan, then stir in the sugar. Set aside to cool completely.

Assemble: Preheat the oven to 200°C (400°F). Line two large baking trays with non-stick baking paper.

Beat the egg in a small bowl to use as an egg wash. Set aside.

Lightly dust your work surface with a little more flour, then remove the pastry from the freezer and roll it out to a 30cm x 40cm (12in x 16in) rectangle.

Using a sharp knife, cut the pastry into 12 squares measuring 10cm (4in). Put the squares on the lined trays, spaced apart.

Brush the edges of each square with the egg wash, making sure you go about 1cm (½in) in. Spoon a small amount of apple filling into the centre of each square. Fold over half of the square diagonally and stick the sides

together to make a triangle. Press the edges together firmly to seal, then crimp the edges with a fork to be extra safe.

Brush the top of each turnover with egg wash. Use the tip of a sharp knife to cut a small hole in the top of each pastry.

Bake: Bake the turnovers in the preheated oven for 17-20 minutes, until puffed up and golden on top.

Let the turnovers cool on the trays for several minutes before moving to a wire rack to cool completely.

Store: In an airtight container at room temperature for up to two days.

Bear paws

Makes 8

For the rough puff pastry:

300g (2½ cups) plain flour, plus extra for dusting

175g (¾ cup) salted butter, cold and cubed

50g (¼ cup) cool water

30g (2 tbsp) salted butter, softened

For the filling:

150g (5¼oz) marzipan

For the egg wash:

1 medium egg, beaten

To decorate:

a handful of flaked almonds

icing sugar, for dusting

I made bear claws in bakery school but found them to be a little too technical when I was deciding which recipes to include in this book. Something a lot easier – and cuter! – are my bear paws: a marzipan-filled puff pastry treat that takes a little bit of time and effort, but with an end result that is too adorable to miss out on!

Make the rough puff pastry: Put the flour and 175g (¾ cup) cold butter in a medium bowl. Using your fingertips, rub the butter into the flour, but leave large chunks of butter that aren't fully incorporated.

Pour in the cool water and bring everything together into a ball. If it's too dry, add a little more water, 1 teaspoon at a time, just until it comes together.

Lightly dust your clean work surface with a little flour. Tip out the dough, then roll it into a small square. Wrap in cling film and pop it in the freezer for 20 minutes.

When you take the dough out of the freezer, lightly dust your work surface with a little flour again. Unwrap the dough, then roll it out into a 20cm x 25cm (8in x 10in) rectangle.

Spread half of the softened butter over the surface of the dough, then cut it in half. Put one half on top of the other half, with the buttered sides pressed together. Wrap in cling film and freeze for another 20 minutes.

Roll the dough out on the lightly floured work surface into a 20cm x 25cm (8in x 10in) rectangle again. Spread the rest of the softened butter over the surface of the rolled dough and cut it in half again. Put one half on top of the other half, with the buttered sides pressed together. Wrap in cling film and freeze for 20 minutes while you make the filling.

Make the filling: Roll the marzipan into eight even-sized balls. Set aside.

Assemble: Preheat the oven to 200°C (400°F). Line two large baking trays with non-stick baking paper.

Lightly dust your work surface with a little flour. Take the pastry out of the freezer, unwrap it and roll it out to a 45cm (18in) square.

Using a large circular cutter (8cm (3¼in) diameter), stamp out 16 circles. Using a mini cutter (I use the large end of a piping nozzle), stamp out 32 mini circles.

Put eight of the large circles on the lined trays. Brush each circle with the egg wash, making sure you go in about 1cm (½in) from the edge all around.

Put a ball of marzipan on top of each round and flatten the ball slightly. Put another pastry circle on top of the marzipan and press the edges together firmly to seal in the marzipan.

Decorate: Put four mini pastry circles at the top of each pastry round to make a paw. Brush the top of each bear paw with egg wash. Put one flaked almond on each of the four mini circles to imitate bear claws.

Bake: Bake the bear paws in the preheated oven for 20–25 minutes, until puffed up and golden on top.

Let the bear paws cool on the trays for a few minutes before transferring to a wire rack. When they are completely cool, dust each one with a little icing sugar.

Store: In an airtight container at room temperature for up to three days.

Jam twists

Makes 10

For the rough puff pastry:

300g (2½ cups) plain flour, plus extra for dusting

175g (¾ cup) salted butter, cold and cubed

50g (¼ cup) cool water

30g (2 tbsp) salted butter, softened

For the filling:

100g (¼ cup) strawberry jam

For the egg wash:

1 medium egg

To decorate:

2 tbsp freeze-dried strawberry powder

These are ideal for using up pastry offcuts, or you can use store-bought ready-rolled pastry. Either way, I can assure you they will disappear in seconds! I get freeze-dried strawberry powder in Tesco, believe it or not. You could also buy whole freeze-dried strawberries and blitz them in a blender or food processor to make a powder.

Make the rough puff pastry: Put the flour and 175g (¾ cup) cold butter in a medium bowl. Using your fingertips, rub the butter into the flour, but leave large chunks of butter that aren't fully incorporated.

Pour in the cool water and bring everything together into a ball. If it's too dry, add a little more water, 1 teaspoon at a time, just until it comes together.

Lightly dust your clean work surface with a little flour. Tip out the dough, then roll it into a small square. Wrap in cling film and pop it in the freezer for 20 minutes.

When you take the dough out of the freezer, lightly dust your work surface with a little flour again. Unwrap the dough, then roll it out into a 20cm x 25cm (8in x 10in) rectangle.

Spread half of the softened butter over the surface of the dough, then cut the dough in half. Put one half on top of the other half, with the buttered sides pressed together. Wrap in cling film and freeze for 20 minutes.

Roll the dough out on the lightly floured work surface into a 20cm x 25cm (8in x 10in) rectangle again. Spread the rest of the softened butter over the surface of the rolled dough and cut it in half again. Once again, put one half on top of the other half, with the buttered sides pressed together. Wrap in cling film and freeze for a final 20 minutes.

Prep: Preheat the oven to 200°C (400°F). Line a large baking tray with non-stick baking paper.

Assemble: Roll out the pastry on your lightly floured work surface to form a 30cm (11¾in) square. Spread the jam across the entire square, going all the way to the edges.

Cut the pastry into 10 strips about 3cm (1¼in) wide. Twist the top of the strand clockwise and the bottom of the strand anticlockwise until the entire strand is tightly twisted and closed. Put the twists on the lined tray, spaced evenly apart.

Egg wash: Beat the egg in a small bowl, then brush the twists with it.

Bake: Bake in the preheated oven for 15–17 minutes, until the twists are puffed up and golden. Let the twists cool on their tray for a few minutes before moving to a wire rack to cool completely.

Decorate: Using a small fine mesh sieve, dust the freeze-dried strawberry powder over the bottom half of each twist.

Store: In an airtight container at room temperature for up to three days.

Blackberry clafoutis

Serves 8

30g (2 tbsp) salted butter, melted

150g (1¼ cups) plain flour

125g (heaped ½ cup) caster sugar

3 medium eggs

250g (1 cup) whole milk

1 tsp vanilla bean paste

For the topping:

125g (4½oz) blackberries

50g (¼ cup) caster sugar

To serve:

vanilla ice cream or warm custard (page 182)

I dream about clafoutis for breakfast every day. I can't make a pancake now without wishing it was a clafoutis instead. Something about its sugary crust, creamy centre and the tangy blackberries won't leave my head. If you make this, I am almost certain it will be one of your favourites too.

Prep: Preheat the oven to 190°C (375°F).

Make the batter: Brush the melted butter all over the base and sides of a large (approx. 30.5cm (12in)) ovenproof frying pan.

Put the flour, sugar, eggs, milk and vanilla in a large mixing bowl. Using an electric mixer, beat until smooth, then pour the batter into the buttered pan.

For the topping: Scatter the blackberries evenly over the top, then sprinkle over the caster sugar.

Bake: Bake in the preheated oven for 30–35 minutes, until the clafoutis is golden brown around the edges and set in the centre.

Serve: Serve with a scoop of vanilla ice cream or with warm custard.

Store: The clafoutis is best eaten on the day it's made, but if you want to make it ahead of time, store the baked clafoutis in the fridge and reheat it in the oven before serving.

Blueberry and custard danishes

Makes 14

For the dough:

600g (5 cups) strong white flour, plus extra for dusting

50g (¼ cup) caster sugar

30g (2 tbsp) salted butter, cold and cubed

1 medium egg

250ml (1 cup) cool water

2 x 7g sachets (5 tsp in total) of fast-action dried yeast

For the lamination:

400g (1¾ cups) salted butter, at room temperature

For the egg wash:

1 medium egg

For the custard:

600g (2½ cups) whole milk

15g (1 tbsp) salted butter

1 tsp vanilla bean paste

200g (1 cup) caster sugar

50g (5 tbsp) cornflour

2 medium eggs

For the topping and glaze:

150g (1 cup) fresh blueberries

2 tbsp apricot jam, warmed

I love how custard and fruit work together in pastries. These danishes feel indulgent but balanced, with the sharpness of the blueberries cutting through the creaminess of the custard. Okay, that all sounds fancy, but these are seriously good.

Make the dough: Put all the dough ingredients in the bowl of a stand mixer fitted with a dough hook (though you can of course knead the dough by hand if you want to). Mix on medium speed for 7–10 minutes, until the dough is smooth and elastic.

Transfer the dough to a lightly floured work surface and roll it out into a rectangle approx. 23cm x 30.5cm (9in x 12in). Wrap it in cling film and refrigerate for at least 3 hours, or overnight for best results.

Prepare the butter slab: Cut the room-temperature butter into thick slices and put them on a sheet of non-stick baking paper. Overlap the slices until you make a rectangle that is 23cm x 30.5cm (9in x 12in). Put another sheet of non-stick baking paper on top of the butter, then gently press the butter together to join the seams. Cut the rectangle back into a 23cm x 30.5cm (9in x 12in) rectangle if any butter has squashed out of place. Wrap the butter slab in the non-stick baking paper and put it flat in the fridge until needed.

Laminate the dough: Once chilled, put the dough on a lightly floured work surface. Remove the butter slab from the fridge.

Roll out the dough lengthwise until it's roughly doubled in size – it should be approx. 61cm (24in) long. Put the butter slab in the middle of the dough.

Fold each end of the dough over the butter so they meet in the middle. Pinch the seam together to seal the dough. Start rolling the dough out horizontally, keeping it the same height but extending the width back to 61cm (24in).

Perform your first fold: Fold one side of the dough two-thirds of the way over itself, then fold the other side on top to create a trifold. Gently press to seal and roll it out once more until it's 61cm (24in) wide.

Perform the second fold: Fold one side halfway over, then fold the other side to meet it. Fold the dough in half once more to create a neat, layered block. Lightly press it down to secure the layers.

Wrap the folded dough tightly in cling film. Put it in the freezer for 30 minutes to rest and chill.

Prove the dough: After chilling, line the largest flat tray you can fit in your oven (or two smaller baking trays) with non-stick baking paper.

Return the dough to a lightly floured work surface. Roll it out into a large rectangle, approx. 41cm x 71cm (16in x 28in), then cut the rectangle into 10cm (4in) squares. You're aiming to make 28 squares.

Using a small round cutter, punch out the centres of half the squares to create 'frames'. Put the full squares on the lined tray, spaced evenly apart.

Beat the egg in a small bowl to use as an egg wash. Brush the squares on the tray with egg wash, then put a cut-out 'frame' square on top of each one. Brush the tops again with egg wash. Adding an egg wash before proving stops the pastry from drying out while it proves and gives it a richer colour after it's baked.

Cover the tray(s) loosely with cling film or a clean tea towel. Allow the dough to prove in a warm, draught-free place for about 2 hours, until it has doubled in size.

Make the custard: Meanwhile, put the milk, butter and vanilla in a large saucepan on a medium heat. Bring to a simmer while whisking constantly, then remove the pan from the heat.

In a separate small bowl, whisk together the sugar, cornflour and eggs until there are no lumps and the sugar has mostly dissolved.

While vigorously whisking the milk mixture in the saucepan, pour in the egg mixture very slowly to prevent the eggs from cooking.

Put the saucepan back on a medium heat and continue to whisk with a wooden spoon until the custard thickens enough to leave a clear line when you run your finger down the back of the spoon.

Let the custard cool completely, then transfer it to a piping bag with no tip. Tie the top of the piping bag to stop the custard from spilling, then put it in the fridge.

Assemble: Preheat the oven to 190°C (375°F).

Give the pastries another full egg wash.

Cut off just the tip of the piping bag of custard. Pipe enough custard to fill the entire cut-out centre of each pastry 'frame'. Put three blueberries on top of the custard on each pastry.

Bake: Bake in the preheated oven for 15–20 minutes, until the pastry is crisp and deep golden.

Make the glaze: Put the apricot jam in a small bowl and warm it in the microwave for 20 seconds (or in a small saucepan on the hob) to melt it until it turns liquid. (Melted apricot jam is the perfect sweet glaze for lots of pastries.)

While the pastries are still warm out of the oven, use a pastry brush to glaze the tops of the pastries with the melted apricot jam. Leave the danishes to cool on their trays.

Store: Keep the danishes in an airtight container in the fridge for up to two days.

Cherry and marzipan scone swirls

Makes 12

400g (3⅓ cups) self-raising flour, plus extra for dusting

25g (1 heaped tbsp) caster sugar

25g (¼ cup) ground almonds

½ tsp baking powder

110g (½ cup) salted butter, diced

180g (¾ cup) buttermilk

500g (1lb 2oz) marzipan

100g (½ cup) glacé cherries, chopped

For the sides:

1 medium egg

a pinch of salt

approx. 75g (¾ cup) flaked almonds

Everyone likes a traditional plain scone, but cherry and almond has been my favourite flavour ever since I first made them for my nana. I couldn't stop thinking about how the basic almond flavour was just an essence added to the dough and how much better marzipan would taste, and voilà, the scone swirl was born.

Prep: Preheat the oven to 180°C (350°F). Line two large baking trays with non-stick baking paper.

Make the scones: Combine the flour, sugar, ground almonds and baking powder in a large bowl. Add the butter and use your fingertips to rub it into the flour mixture until it resembles breadcrumbs.

Make a well in the centre of the bowl and pour in the buttermilk. Using one hand held like a claw and keeping your other hand clean, mix with your claw hand just until it comes together into a dough.

Lightly dust a clean work surface with a little flour, then tip out the dough. Gently knead the dough just to bring it together, then roll it out into a rectangle about 1cm (½in) thick and measuring 20cm x 30cm (8in x 12in). Lightly brush the top with water. This will help the marzipan stick to the dough. Set aside.

Tear off a large sheet of non-stick baking paper, then put the block of marzipan on it. Tear off a second sheet and put it on top of the marzipan, then roll it out between the two sheets of paper until it's the same size as your rectangle of scone dough.

Make the swirls: Put the marzipan on top of the dough, then give it a light roll with the rolling pin to help the marzipan stick. Scatter the chopped cherries across the marzipan. Starting with the longest side of the dough, roll it up tightly into a cylinder, like a cinnamon roll.

Egg wash: Beat the egg with a pinch of salt, then brush the top of the roll all over with the egg wash. Slice the roll into 12 pieces about 2.5cm (1in) thick.

Gently pat flaked almonds onto the egg-washed sides, then put the scones on the lined baking trays, spaced apart to give them room to expand.

Bake: Bake in the preheated oven for 20–25 minutes, until the scones are golden around the edges and the centre looks dry. Let the scone swirls set on the trays until they're cool enough to handle, then transfer to a wire rack to cool completely.

Store: In an airtight container at room temperature for up to three days.

Frog doughnuts

For the doughnuts:

275g (1 cup + 2 tbsp) whole milk

500g (4¼ cups) strong white flour, plus extra for dusting

100g (½ cup) caster sugar

110g (½ cup) salted butter, cold and cubed

1 medium egg, beaten

1 x 7g sachet (2¼ tsp) of fast-action dried yeast

For the egg wash:

1 medium egg

For the filling:

2 large cooking apples, such as Bramley

50g (¼ cup) caster sugar

To serve:

warm custard (page 182) or cinnamon sugar

Frog doughnuts are the most viral recipe I have ever created, with more than 10 million views across all my social platforms. These charming doughnuts are as adorable as they are delicious.

Prep: Line two large baking trays with non-stick baking paper.

Make the dough: Pour the milk into a small saucepan on a medium heat and let it get lukewarm (or you can warm it in the microwave for 30–45 seconds). You should be able to comfortably dip your finger in it. Set aside.

Put the flour and sugar in a large bowl and stir to combine. Add the butter, then use your fingertips to rub it into the flour and sugar until it has a breadcrumb consistency.

Make a well in the centre of the bowl and pour in the warm milk, beaten egg and yeast.

Stir together with a wooden spoon until a shaggy dough forms, then knead it with your hands for about 10 minutes, until a smooth, elastic dough forms. You can of course do this with a stand mixer fitted with a dough hook instead.

Tip the dough out onto a lightly floured work surface. Using a sharp knife, cut it into 14 evenly sized pieces. Roll each piece into a smooth ball using the palm of your hand.

Put 10 balls on the lined trays, spaced evenly apart.

Cut the remaining four balls into 20 small rounds (these are the eyes) and 40 small cylinders (these are the legs).

Egg wash: Beat the egg in a small bowl. Brush all 10 doughnuts with the egg wash, then stick four legs and two eyes onto each doughnut. Lightly brush the legs and eyes with egg wash too.

Prove the dough: Loosely cover the doughnuts with clean tea towels, then put them in a warm, draught-free place for 1–2 hours, until they have doubled in size.

Bake: Preheat the oven to 190°C (375°F).

Bake the doughnuts in the preheated oven for 25–30 minutes, until they are dark golden on the outside and the bottoms of the doughnuts sound hollow when tapped.

Let the doughnuts cool on wire racks.

Make the filling: Meanwhile, peel, core and dice the apples into very small pieces (you could also grate them).

Using a medium saucepan, add just enough water to cover the base, then add the apples and put the pan on a medium-high heat. Bring to a boil, then reduce the heat and cook, stirring, until the apples have completely softened to mush.

Put a fine mesh sieve on top of a bowl. Pour the softened apples into the sieve, then rub it through the mesh with the back of a spoon to remove any lumps. Stir in the sugar to taste (you don't have to use all of it). Allow the filling to cool completely.

Assemble: Fit a piping bag with a doughnut filling tip (or you can use a circle tip and cut a small hole in the bottom of each doughnut). Pour the apple filling into the piping bag, then fill each doughnut centre with the apple purée. The best place to fill from is the base of the doughnut at the back, pointing the piping tip towards the front of the doughnut.

Serve: Serve the doughnuts with warm custard or dipped into cinnamon sugar.

Store: In an airtight container at room temperature for up to two days.

COOKIES & BISCUITS

Button cookies

Makes 12

250g (1 cup + 2 tbsp) salted
butter, softened

350g (1¾ cups) caster sugar

30g (2 tbsp) light brown sugar

2 medium eggs

1 tsp vanilla bean paste

400g (3⅓ cups) plain flour

½ tsp baking powder

To decorate:

1–2 handfuls of colourful
chocolate candies, such as
Smarties or M&Ms

My mum never lets me forget the time I was about eight years old and had a friend over after school. We decided to make button cookies, but didn't account for the huge amount we were making. My mum was shoving the cookies in and out of the oven long after my friend and I got bored and left the kitchen. Sorry, Mum! I promise I wrote this recipe to make a normal number of cookies.

Make the dough: Using an electric mixer, beat the butter and sugars together in a large mixing bowl for a few minutes, until pale and fluffy.

Add the eggs one at a time, beating until fully incorporated before adding the next egg. Stir in the vanilla.

Sift in the flour and baking powder and mix just until a dough forms.

Using your hands, form the dough into 12 balls a bit bigger than a golf ball (approx. 80g (2¾oz) each).

Put the balls in a plastic tub and cover it with a lid or put them on a tray and cover them in cling film, then pop in the freezer for 30 minutes.

Prep: Preheat the oven to 190°C (375°F). Line two large baking trays with non-stick baking paper.

Bake: Put six balls on each tray, spaced well apart so they have room to spread. Bake in the preheated oven for 12–15 minutes, until the cookies are a deep golden-brown colour around the edges and pale golden in the centre. If you want a crisp, crunchy cookie, bake them in the oven for a few minutes longer, until the centre is a deep golden colour.

As soon as you remove the cookies from the oven, press a few chocolate candies on top of each one.

To get perfectly round cookies that are all the same size, grab a glass, mug or small bowl that's a little bigger than the cookies. While the cookies are still hot from the oven, put it upside down over a cookie, then gently swirl it around a few times. Lift up the glass or bowl and voilà, a perfect circle! Repeat with the remaining cookies.

Let the cookies cool on the trays for several minutes after you've shaped them, then transfer the cookies to a wire rack to firm up fully.

Store: In an airtight container at room temperature for up to three days.

Chocolate cherry cookies

Makes 10

150g (⅔ cup) salted butter, softened

150g (¾ cup) caster sugar

100g (heaped ½ cup) light brown sugar

1 medium egg

1 tsp vanilla bean paste

250g (2 cups) plain flour

30g (¼ cup) cocoa powder

1 tsp baking powder

100g (3½oz) dark chocolate, cut into chunks

10 teaspoons cherry jam

When developing this recipe, I tried every variation of cherries, from glacé to fresh, but nothing beat the blob of jam. For such an impressive-looking cookie, you'd never guess how easy they are to make.

Prep: Line two large baking trays with non-stick baking paper.

Make the dough: Using an electric mixer, beat the butter and sugars together in a large mixing bowl for a few minutes, until pale and fluffy.

Add the egg and vanilla and beat until combined.

Sift in the flour, cocoa powder and baking powder. Mix until the dough is smooth and there are no dry lumps. Add the dark chocolate chunks and mix until they are evenly distributed in the dough.

Roll the cookie dough into 10 golf ball-sized balls and put them on the lined trays. Using your thumb, make a large well in the centre of each ball. Fill each well with a teaspoon of cherry jam.

Freeze the cookie dough balls for 20 minutes.

Bake: Preheat the oven to 180°C (350°F).

Put five balls on each tray, spaced well apart so they have room to spread. Bake the cookies in the preheated oven for 15–18 minutes, until the edges are crisp but the centre is still slightly gooey.

To get perfectly round cookies that are all the same size, grab a glass, mug or small bowl that's a little bigger than the cookies. While the cookies are still hot from the oven, put it upside down over a cookie, then gently swirl it around a few times. Lift up the glass or bowl and voilà, a perfect circle! Repeat with the remaining cookies.

Let the cookies cool on the trays for several minutes after you've shaped them, then transfer the cookies to a wire rack to firm up fully.

Store: In an airtight container at room temperature for up to three days.

Chocolate chip shortbread

Makes 15

200g (¾ cup + 2 tbsp) salted butter, softened

100g (½ cup) caster sugar

200g (1⅔ cups) plain flour

100g (½ cup) chocolate chips

I love shortbread for its simplicity, but adding chocolate chips is never a bad idea. These soft, buttery fingers are the kind of biscuit you keep reaching for despite yourself.

Prep: Preheat the oven to 190°C (375°F). Line an 18cm x 28cm (7in x 11in) or 23cm (9in) square baking tin with non-stick baking paper, letting the paper overhang the sides so that you can use it to lift the shortbread out of the tin later.

Make the dough: Using an electric mixer, beat the butter and sugar together in a large mixing bowl for a few minutes, until pale and fluffy.

Stir in the flour and chocolate chips and mix just until it all comes together into a dough.

Tip the dough into the lined tin and spread it out evenly into the corners. Using the tip of a sharp knife, lightly score the dough into 15 fingers, then prick the centre of each finger vertically with a fork.

Bake: Bake in the preheated oven for 15–20 minutes, until the shortbread is golden brown on top.

While the shortbread is still very warm, slice it into 15 pieces along the lines you scored. Leave the fingers in the tray to cool for several minutes before using the overhanging paper to lift them out of the tray and onto a wire rack to cool completely.

Store: In an airtight container at room temperature for up to five days.

Funfetti whoopie pies

Makes 12

150g (⅔ cup) salted butter, softened

125g (heaped ½ cup) caster sugar

2 medium eggs

1 tsp vanilla bean paste

275g (2¼ cups) plain flour

1 tsp baking powder

a small handful of bake-stable rainbow sprinkles, plus extra to decorate

For the filling:

120g (1 cup) icing sugar

110g (½ cup) salted butter, softened

The first cookbook I ever bought with my pocket money was a book on whoopie pies, so I couldn't resist including my own recipe for ones with my funfetti twist! These soft sandwich cookies are sure to make anyone smile when you serve them.

Prep: Preheat the oven to 180°C (350°F). Line two large baking trays with non-stick baking paper.

Make the dough: Using an electric mixer, beat the butter and sugar together in a large mixing bowl for a few minutes, until pale and fluffy.

Add the eggs and vanilla and beat until combined.

Sift in the flour and baking powder, then mix just until a dough is formed. Mix through the bake-stable sprinkles until they are evenly dispersed in the dough.

Using your hands, divide the dough into 24 balls measuring 2.5cm (1in) in diameter and put them on the lined baking trays, spaced well apart to give them room to spread. Press them down slightly with the palm of your hand.

Bake: Bake in the preheated oven for 10–12 minutes, until they are golden brown around the edges and they spring back when lightly pressed. Let the cookies cool completely on the trays.

Make the filling: Meanwhile, sift the icing sugar into a medium bowl and add the butter. Using an electric mixer, beat together until very pale. This can take up to 10 minutes. If the buttercream is very stiff, add a few tablespoons of cool water and continue to beat.

Assemble: Make sure the cookies are completely cool before you assemble the whoopie pies, otherwise the buttercream will melt. Gently peel the cookies off the lined baking trays and turn half of them upside down.

Using a small spoon, scoop 1 heaped tablespoon of buttercream on top of each of the upside-down cookies. Put the remaining pies on top of the iced ones and gently press them down to sandwich them together with the buttercream.

Decorate: Pour a small handful of rainbow sprinkles onto a clean plate. Roll the sides of the whoopie pies in the sprinkles so they stick to the buttercream.

Store: In an airtight container at room temperature for up to three days.

Garibaldi biscuits

200g (1⅔ cups) self-raising flour

60g (⅓ cup) light brown sugar

60g (4 tbsp) salted butter, cold and cubed

30g (2 tbsp) whole milk

1 medium egg, beaten

100g (⅔ cup) currants or raisins

30g (1½ tbsp) granulated sugar

Garibaldis aren't a nickname for a bald man called Gary – they are an old-fashioned biscuit that lets the dried fruit do all the work (currants are traditional in Garibaldi biscuits, but I prefer raisins, which are sweeter). Having no crazy extras can be quite satisfying when you're looking for a simple biscuit to dunk into a cup of tea.

Prep: Preheat the oven to 190°C (375°F). Line an 18cm x 28cm (7in x 11in) or 23cm (9in) square baking tin with non-stick baking paper, letting the paper overhang the sides so that you can use it to lift the biscuits out of the tin at the end.

Make the dough: Put the flour and brown sugar in a medium bowl and stir to combine, then add the butter. Using your fingertips, rub the butter into the flour mixture until a breadcrumb consistency is formed.

Add the milk and most of the beaten egg (set a small bit aside for egg wash) and knead just until it comes together into a soft dough. Add the currants or raisins and knead again just until they are evenly distributed throughout the dough. Press the dough into the lined tin, spreading it to a flat, even thickness throughout.

Brush the reserved egg wash all over, then sprinkle the granulated sugar evenly across the surface of the dough.

Bake: Bake in the preheated oven for 13–15 minutes, until the biscuit is golden on top and crisp.

Let the slab cool in the tin for several minutes, then use the paper to lift it out of the tin and onto a chopping board. Cut into 12 biscuits.

Store: In an airtight container at room temperature for up to three days.

Gingerbread and white chocolate cookies

Makes 10

200g (¾ cup + 2 tbsp) salted butter, softened

250g (1½ cups) light brown sugar

2 medium eggs

1 tsp vanilla bean paste

450g (3¾ cups) plain flour

2 tbsp ground ginger

1 tsp ground cinnamon

1 tsp baking powder

150g (5¼oz) white chocolate, broken into chunks (set 50g (1¾oz) aside for topping)

Warm gingerbread with milky white chocolate ... just writing that is making me drool. Sweet and spicy paired in a light cookie – what more could you want?

Prep: Line two large baking trays with non-stick baking paper.

Make the dough: Using an electric mixer, beat the butter and sugar together in a large mixing bowl for a few minutes, until pale and fluffy.

Add the eggs and vanilla and beat until combined.

Sift in the flour, ginger, cinnamon and baking powder, then mix just until there are no dry spots in the dough.

Add 100g (3½oz) of the white chocolate chunks and knead them in just until they are evenly distributed throughout the dough.

Roll the dough into 10 golf ball-sized balls and divide them between the lined trays, spaced evenly apart to give them room to spread out during baking. Press the remaining 50g (1¾oz) of white chocolate chunks into the tops of the balls. Freeze the cookie dough for 20 minutes.

Bake: Preheat the oven to 180°C (350°F).

Bake the cookies in the preheated oven for 15–18 minutes, until they are golden and crisp around the edges but still slightly gooey in the centre.

Gently press the top of each cookie with a flat surface (I use the base of a small bowl). This improves the appearance of the cookie but it isn't strictly necessary.

To get perfectly round cookies that are all the same size, grab a glass, mug or small bowl that's a little bigger than the cookies. While the cookies are still hot from the oven, put it upside down over a cookie, then gently swirl it around a few times. Lift up the glass or bowl and voilà, a perfect circle! Repeat with the remaining cookies.

Let the cookies cool on their trays for several minutes before moving them to a wire rack to cool completely.

Store: In an airtight container at room temperature for up to three days.

Lemon and raspberry biscotti

Makes 8–10

200g (1⅔ cups) plain flour, plus extra for dusting

100g (1 cup) ground almonds

75g (⅓ cup) caster sugar

75g (heaped ⅓ cup) light brown sugar

1 tsp baking powder

a pinch of salt

2 medium eggs

zest of 1 lemon

20g (1 heaped tbsp) freeze-dried raspberry powder

To decorate:

100g (3½oz) white chocolate, melted

freeze-dried raspberry pieces

These biscotti are a cheerful twist on a classic. With their pop of colour and satisfying crunch, they're the kind of bake that feels just as at home in a biscuit tin as they do wrapped up for gifting: simple to make and a joy to share.

Prep: Preheat the oven to 180°C (350°F). Line a baking tray with non-stick baking paper.

Make the dough: Put the flour, ground almonds, both sugars, baking powder, salt and eggs in a large bowl and mix until fully combined.

Divide the dough into two equal halves and put each half in a separate mixing bowl.

Add the lemon zest to one bowl and mix it into the dough. Add the freeze-dried raspberry powder to the other bowl and mix it into the dough.

On a lightly floured work surface, roll the lemon dough into a 15cm x 20cm (6in x 8in) rectangle. Do the same with the raspberry dough.

Put the raspberry dough on top of the lemon dough and cut it in half vertically so that you now have two rectangles. Put one rectangle on the lined tray, then stack the other one on top of it and smoosh them down slightly into an oval shape. This will make four stripes in the dough.

Bake: Bake in the preheated oven for 20–25 minutes, until just crisp on the outside.

Remove the baked biscotti from the oven and turn the temperature down to 160°C (325°F).

Slice the oval into 8–10 long pieces that are 2.5cm (1in) wide, cutting slightly diagonally to give the biscotti a nice shape.

Put the biscotti back on the lined tray, cut sides up, and bake in the oven for another 15–20 minutes, until golden brown on the edges and crisp to the touch. Let the biscotti cool completely on wire racks.

Decorate: Line a baking tray with non-stick baking paper.

In a small microwave-safe bowl, melt the white chocolate in the microwave in 30-second increments, stirring after each one. Or you can put the chocolate in a heatproof bowl set on top of a saucepan of gently simmering water, making sure the water doesn't touch the bottom of the bowl, and melt it that way.

Working with one biscuit at a time, dip one end into the melted chocolate. Put the dipped biscotti on the lined baking tray, then sprinkle a pinch of freeze-dried raspberry pieces onto the melted chocolate.

When all the biscotti have been decorated, put the tray in the fridge to allow the chocolate to set, then remove the biscotti from the fridge (they will get soft if stored in the fridge for too long).

Store: In an airtight container at room temperature for up to three days.

Mint and dark chocolate cookies

Makes 10

150g (⅔ cup) salted butter, softened

150g (¾ cup) caster sugar

100g (heaped ½ cup) light brown sugar

1 medium egg

1 tsp green food colouring

½ tsp peppermint extract

250g (2 cups) plain flour

1 tsp baking powder

100g (3½oz) dark chocolate, cut into chunks

The best ice cream flavour, but in cookie form! I add food colouring to make them green to prevent any confusion for all the mint-chocolate haters, but it also adds a bit of fun to an otherwise normal cookie.

Prep: Line two large baking trays with non-stick baking paper.

Make the dough: Using an electric mixer, beat the butter and sugars together in a large mixing bowl for a few minutes, until pale and fluffy.

Beat in the egg, food colouring and peppermint extract.

Sift in the flour and baking powder and mix just until there are no dry spots left in the dough.

Add the chocolate chunks and mix until they are evenly distributed throughout the dough.

Roll the dough into 10 even-sized balls (they should be a bit bigger than a golf ball). Divide the balls between the two lined trays and freeze for at least 20 minutes.

Bake: Preheat the oven to 180°C (350°F).

Make sure the balls are spaced well apart to give the cookies room to spread. Bake in the preheated oven for 15–20 minutes, until the cookies are slightly golden around the edges and the base, but still a little gooey in the centre.

To get perfectly round cookies that are all the same size, grab a glass, mug or small bowl that's a little bigger than the cookies. While the cookies are still hot from the oven, put it upside down over a cookie, then gently swirl it around a few times. Lift up the glass or bowl and voilà, a perfect circle! Repeat with the remaining cookies.

Allow the cookies to cool on their trays for several minutes after you've shaped them before moving them to a wire rack to cool completely.

Store: In an airtight container at room temperature for up to three days.

Ooey gooey cookies

Makes 8

110g (½ cup) salted butter, softened

120g (¾ cup) light brown sugar

120g (heaped ½ cup) caster sugar

1 medium egg

1 tsp vanilla bean paste

250g (2 cups) plain flour

1 tsp baking soda

½ tsp baking powder

100g (3½oz) dark chocolate, cut into chunks

8 tbsp chocolate spread

To finish:

a pinch of flaky sea salt (optional)

A good cookie recipe is almost a requirement to call yourself a baker. This one is mine: chocolatey and soft in the middle but with a bit of crunch on the outer edges. Enjoy your cookies warm from the oven – with a glass of milk, of course.

Prep: Line two large baking trays with non-stick baking paper.

Make the dough: Using an electric mixer, beat the butter and sugars together in a large mixing bowl for a few minutes, until pale and fluffy.

Add the egg and vanilla and beat until combined.

Sift in the flour, baking soda and baking powder, then stir just until a dough forms. Knead the dough with your hands in the bowl until almost all the flour has been combined. Add the chocolate chunks and knead until the dough is smooth and there are no dry spots.

Divide the dough into eight even pieces, then roll into balls the size of golf balls. With your fingers, create a deep well in the centre of each ball. Add 1 tablespoon of chocolate spread to the well, then close the well back over with the cookie dough, making sure the chocolate spread is completely enclosed. I like to leave a few chocolate chunks sticking out of the surface of the cookies because when chocolate is put on top of a cookie and melts in the oven, it looks really good. Put each ball on one lined tray, seam side down.

When all the cookie dough balls are filled with chocolate spread, put the tray in the freezer for 30 minutes or in the fridge for 1 hour.

Bake: Preheat the oven to 190°C (375°F).

Divide the balls between the two lined trays, spaced apart to give them room to spread. Bake in the preheated oven for 10–12 minutes, until the edges are crisp and golden and the centres are still slightly gooey.

To get perfectly round cookies that are all the same size, grab a glass, mug or small bowl that's a little bigger than the cookies. While the cookies are still hot from the oven, put it upside down over a cookie, then gently swirl it around a few times. Lift up the glass or bowl and voilà, a perfect circle! Repeat with the remaining cookies.

Let the cookies cool on their trays for a few minutes after you've shaped them before moving them to a wire rack.

To finish: Sprinkle each cookie with a small pinch of flaky sea salt (if using) while they're still warm.

Store: In an airtight container at room temperature for up to three days.

Peanut butter and chocolate swirl cookies

Makes 8

110g (½ cup) salted butter, softened

100g (heaped ½ cup) light brown sugar

100g (½ cup) caster sugar

100g (scant ½ cup) crunchy peanut butter

1 medium egg

1 tsp vanilla bean paste

180g (1½ cups) plain flour

1 tsp baking powder

20g (2 tbsp) cocoa powder

Peanut butter and chocolate is a combination I will never get tired of! These swirly cookies are a staple in my baking rotation and are the perfect treat when you're craving something that's not too sweet.

Prep: Line two large baking trays with non-stick baking paper.

Make the dough: Using an electric mixer, beat together the butter, both sugars, peanut butter, egg and vanilla in a large mixing bowl until well combined.

Sift in the flour and baking powder and mix until a dough forms.

Divide the dough into two equal halves. Transfer one half of the dough to a separate mixing bowl, add the cocoa powder and knead it in until smooth. Add 2 tablespoons of cool water to the cocoa powder dough if it seems too dry.

Put the chocolate dough back in the large bowl with the other dough. Tear the doughs apart and start to randomly swirl them together. You don't need to be too fussy – just mix them together until the dough looks slightly marbled.

Divide the dough into eight golf ball-sized pieces and put them on one lined tray. Freeze for 25 minutes.

Bake: Preheat the oven to 180°C (350°F).

Divide the chilled dough balls between the two lined trays, spaced well apart. Bake in the preheated oven for 13–15 minutes, until golden brown around the edges.

To get perfectly round cookies that are all the same size, grab a glass, mug or small bowl that's a little bigger than the cookies. While the cookies are still hot from the oven, put it upside down over a cookie, then gently swirl it around a few times. Lift up the glass or bowl and voilà, a perfect circle! Repeat with the remaining cookies.

Let the cookies cool on their trays for a few minutes after you've shaped them before moving to a wire rack.

Store: In an airtight container at room temperature for up to three days.

Spooky spiced skellies

Makes 10–12

110g (½ cup) salted butter

125g (¾ cup) light brown sugar

80g (4 tbsp) golden syrup

300g (2½ cups) plain flour, plus extra for dusting

1 tbsp ground ginger

1 tsp ground cinnamon

1 tsp ground nutmeg

½ tsp baking powder

To decorate:

100g (¾ cup) icing sugar

1–2 tbsp cool water

Why is gingerbread only eaten at Christmastime? Warm spiced biscuits feel much more autumnal to me. These are spooky but not very scary, perfect for Halloween.

Prep: Preheat the oven to 190°C (375°F). Line two large baking trays with non-stick baking paper.

Make the dough: Put the butter, brown sugar and golden syrup in a medium saucepan on a medium heat and melt together (or you can do this in the microwave).

Add the flour, ginger, cinnamon, nutmeg and baking powder. Beat with a spoon until a dough forms. If the dough is very crumbly, add a few teaspoons of cool water and knead again until it comes together. Tip the dough out onto a clean work surface, wrap it in cling film and refrigerate for 30 minutes.

Make the shapes: On a lightly floured surface, roll out the gingerbread dough until it's slightly thicker than a euro coin (about 5mm (¼in) thick).

Using a gingerbread man-shaped cutter (or any other shape you like), stamp out as many gingerbread men as you can. Gather up the scraps, then roll out the dough again and stamp out more gingerbread men – depending on the size of your cutter, you should get between 10 and 12. Space the biscuits out on the lined trays.

Bake: Bake in the preheated oven for 12–15 minutes, until the gingerbread men are a deep golden brown.

Cool on the trays before transferring to a wire rack to cool completely.

Decorate: Put the icing sugar in a small bowl with just enough cool water to bring it to a soft paste. Keep the icing thick enough to pipe. Transfer the icing to a piping bag, then snip the very tip of the piping bag to create as small a hole as possible.

On each gingerbread man, pipe the skeleton bones as shown in the photo. Leave the icing to set completely before serving.

Store: In an airtight container at room temperature for up to three days.

Strawberry mallow and coconut rounds

Makes 12

For the strawberry mallow:

8 gelatine leaves

100g (⅓ cup + 4 tsp) cool water

200g (1 cup) caster sugar

100g (5 tbsp) glucose syrup

75g (⅔ cup) icing sugar

2 tbsp freeze-dried strawberry powder

For the biscuits:

450g (3¾ cups) plain flour, plus extra for dusting

200g (1½ cups) cornflour

200g (¾ cup + 2 tbsp) salted butter, cold and cubed

150g (¾ cup) caster sugar

2 medium eggs

1 tsp vanilla bean paste

To finish:

100g (¼ cup) strawberry jam

100g (1¼ cups) desiccated coconut

If you say the words 'marshmallow' and 'coconut' in the same sentence, you are sure to see me run towards you as fast as lightning. Growing up, my favourite biscuits were a combination of just that. 'Strawberry mallow and coconut rounds' is a mouthful to say, but also a mouthful of pure bliss to eat.

Make the marshmallow: Using a medium metal or heatproof glass mixing bowl (do not use plastic), scald the bowl with very hot water, then dry it completely. Put about 3 tablespoons of tap water in the bowl, then add the gelatine and stir gently. Set aside.

Pour the 100g (⅓ cup + 4 tsp) of cool water into a medium saucepan on a high heat. Add the caster sugar and glucose syrup. Bring to a boil, stirring continuously until all the sugar has dissolved.

Use a sugar thermometer to measure the temperature, making sure it's not touching the bottom of the saucepan. When the boiling mixture reaches 105°C–110°C (221°F–230°F), remove the pan from the heat and set it aside for a few minutes.

When the sugar mixture has cooled slightly, pour it over the gelatine mixture. Using an electric mixer, beat together on a high speed for 6–10 minutes, until medium peaks form and the mixture is glossy and white. Add the icing sugar and strawberry powder and beat until completely combined.

Put a 1cm (½in) circle piping tip into a piping bag, then spoon in the marshmallow mixture. Put the filled piping bag in the fridge to chill.

Make the biscuits: Line two large baking trays with non-stick baking paper.

Put the flour and cornflour in a medium bowl and whisk to combine. Add the butter and use your fingertips to rub it in until it's the consistency of breadcrumbs.

Add the sugar, eggs and vanilla and mix until a soft dough forms. If the mixture is too dry, add a few teaspoons of cool water. Tip the dough out and bring it into a ball, then wrap it in cling film and put it in the fridge for 20–30 minutes to allow the butter to solidify again.

Roll out the chilled dough on a lightly floured work surface until it's just under 1cm (½in) thick. Using a medium circle cutter, stamp out 24 circles. Then, with a much smaller circle cutter (I use the wide end of a circle piping tip), stamp out the centre of each circle.

Put all the biscuits on one lined baking tray and put it in the freezer for 20 minutes.

Bake: Preheat the oven to 190°C (375°F).

Divide the chilled biscuits evenly between the two lined trays, spaced well apart to give them room to spread. Bake in the preheated oven for 8–10 minutes, until golden brown around the edges and crisp.

Let the biscuits cool for a few minutes on their trays, then transfer to a wire rack to cool completely before filling.

Assemble: Spread the jam across the bottom of each biscuit. Arrange the biscuits with the jam side facing up and set aside half of them for the tops.

Pipe small blobs of strawberry marshmallow around the edges of 12 biscuits. Put one of the reserved biscuits on top of the marshmallow, jam side down, and gently sandwich them together.

Spread the desiccated coconut over a large plate. Roll the sides of the filled biscuits in the coconut, allowing it to stick to the marshmallow sides.

Store: In an airtight container in the fridge for up to three days.

TRAYBAKES & BARS

Apple custard pudding cake

Serves 12

200g (¾ cup + 2 tbsp) salted butter, softened

300g (1½ cups) caster sugar

3 medium eggs

400g (3⅓ cups) self-raising flour

1½ tsp baking powder

2 large Bramley apples (approx. 350g/12oz), peeled, cored and cut into small chunks

100g (⅔ cup) custard (I make it using custard powder, but if you want to use homemade, use the recipe on page 182)

In late August, when Bramley apples are ready to be picked, I make this cake to use up as many as I can. I noticed I was pairing every apple cake with custard but was spending so much time making it from scratch that I wouldn't eat the cake if I didn't feel like making custard too. That's where this recipe comes to the rescue: the custard and the apple are together in the cake for convenience as much as for the unbeatable flavour pairing.

Prep: Preheat the oven to 180°C (350°F). Line an 18cm x 28cm (7in x 11in) or 23cm (9in) square baking tin with non-stick baking paper, letting the paper overhang the sides so that you can use it to lift the cake out of the tin at the end.

Make the cake: Using an electric mixer, beat the butter and sugar together in a large mixing bowl for a few minutes, until pale and fluffy.

Add the eggs and beat until fully combined.

Sift in the flour and baking powder. Fold through until there are no dry lumps left and the batter is smooth.

Add the diced apple chunks and stir until they are spread evenly throughout the batter.

Pour the batter into the lined tin, spreading it evenly into the corners.

Make the custard: If you're using custard powder, like I do, make up 100g (⅔ cup) according to the packet instructions, then spread the custard across the top of the batter.

Bake: Bake the cake in the middle of the preheated oven for about 1 hour, until it's golden on top and a skewer inserted into the middle comes out clean.

Serve: Let the cake cool completely in the tin before using the paper to lift it out, then cut it into 12 squares.

Store: In an airtight container at room temperature for up to three days.

Banoffee traybake

Serves 12

For the syrup and topping:

80g (4 tbsp) golden syrup

60g (4 tbsp) salted butter, melted

30g (2 tbsp) light brown sugar

2 large bananas, peeled and thinly sliced into rounds

For the cake:

200g (¾ cup + 2 tbsp) salted butter, softened

350g (2 cups) light brown sugar

2 large bananas, peeled

3 medium eggs

270g (2¼ cups) self-raising flour

1 tsp ground cinnamon

To serve:

whipped cream, warm custard (page 182) or vanilla ice cream

Did you know that when you bake bananas, they can turn pink? Yep, it happens! I absolutely love banoffee but prefer a cake rather than a tart, so for me, this is the best of both banoffee worlds.

Prep: Preheat the oven to 180°C (350°F). Line an 18cm x 28cm (7in x 11in) or 23cm (9in) square baking tin with non-stick baking paper, letting the paper overhang the sides so that you can use it to lift the cake out of the tin at the end.

Make the syrup and topping: Put the golden syrup, melted butter and light brown sugar in a small bowl and stir together into a thick paste. Spread this paste evenly across the base of the lined tin.

Put the banana slices on top of the buttery paste. Keep the slices flat and make sure none of the slices are overlapping. Set aside.

Make the cake: Using an electric mixer, beat the butter and sugar in a large mixing bowl for a few minutes, until pale and fluffy.

Lightly crush the peeled bananas with a fork, then add them to the bowl along with the eggs and mix until combined.

Sift in the flour and cinnamon and fold until there are no dry spots of flour left.

Gently spoon the cake batter into the tin, being careful not to mix the batter with the banana slices and syrup on the base. Smooth the top of the cake.

Bake: Bake in the preheated oven for 35–40 minutes, until golden brown on top and a skewer inserted into the middle comes out clean.

Let the cake cool in the tin for several minutes before inverting it onto a serving plate so that the sliced bananas that were on the base of the tin are now on the top. Carefully peel the baking paper off the top, then slice the cake into 12 squares.

Serve: Serve with a dollop of whipped cream, some warm custard or a scoop of vanilla ice cream.

Store: In an airtight container at room temperature for up to two days.

Blueberry crumble cake

Serves 12

For the cake:

180g (heaped 1 cup) fresh or frozen blueberries (thawed and patted dry if frozen)

225g (1 cup) salted butter, softened

450g (2¼ cups) caster sugar

3 medium eggs

140g (½ cup + 4 tsp) buttermilk

1 tsp vanilla bean paste

550g (4½ cups) plain flour, plus extra for dusting the blueberries

2 tsp baking powder

For the crumble:

150g (1¼ cups) plain flour

110g (½ cup) salted butter, cold and cubed

50g (¼ cup) caster sugar

2 tbsp ground cinnamon

Whenever we had blueberries in the fridge that were starting to take a turn, I would make this crumble cake for a sweet breakfast. It became a favourite in my family and before I knew it, I was buying blueberries specifically to make it.

You can use other berries and fruits in this recipe – raspberries, pitted cherries, cubed pears, diced apple or rhubarb all work well.

Prep: Preheat the oven to 190°C (375°F). Line an 18cm x 28cm (7in x 11in) or 23cm (9in) square baking tin with non-stick baking paper.

Make the cake: Wash the blueberries, discarding any stems, and pat them dry. Put them in a bowl, add 1 tablespoon of flour and toss them gently to coat. The flour helps prevent the blueberries sinking to the bottom of the cake.

Using an electric mixer, beat the butter and sugar together in a medium mixing bowl for a few minutes, until pale and fluffy.

Add the eggs, buttermilk and vanilla and beat until fully combined.

Sift in the flour and baking powder. Gently fold to incorporate the flour into a smooth batter. Pour the batter into the lined tray and set aside.

Make the crumble topping: Put all the crumble ingredients in a small bowl. Using your fingertips, rub the butter into the dry ingredients until the mixture forms large clumps. Scatter the crumble mixture evenly across the top of the cake batter.

Bake: Bake in the preheated oven for 45–50 minutes, until golden on top and a skewer inserted into the middle comes out clean.

Serve: This cake can't be turned out of the tin, so allow it to cool completely in the tin, then cut into 12 pieces and remove the slices from the tin one by one. This keeps the crumble from falling off the cake and making a mess!

Store: In an airtight container at room temperature for up to three days.

Carrot layer cake

Serves 12

For the cake:

3 large carrots, peeled and grated

300g (1¾ cups) light brown sugar

3 medium eggs

250g (1 cup) vegetable oil

zest and juice of 1 small orange

1 tsp vanilla bean paste

400g (3⅓ cups) plain flour

5 tbsp ground cinnamon

2 tbsp mixed spice

1 tbsp ground nutmeg

2 tsp ground ginger

2 tsp baking powder

For the cream cheese icing:

600g (1lb 5oz) cream cheese

200g (1⅔ cups) icing sugar

140g (½ cup + 2 tbsp) salted butter, softened

1 tsp ground cinnamon

To decorate:

100g (1 cup) walnuts, chopped into small pieces

I count a slice of carrot cake as one of my five a day. I could write a poem about how much I love this cake, but I'll spare you and let the photo do all the talking instead.

Prep: Preheat the oven to 190°C (375°F). Line an 18cm x 28cm (7in x 11in) or 23cm (9in) square baking tin with non-stick baking paper, letting the paper overhang the sides so that you can use it to lift the cake out of the tin later.

Prepare the carrots: Put the grated carrots in the centre of a clean tea towel. Bring the four corners of the towel together, then twist and squeeze over a sink to drain off as much water from the carrots as possible. Put the grated carrots in a bowl and set aside.

Make the cake: Using an electric mixer, beat the sugar, eggs, oil, orange zest and juice and vanilla in a large mixing bowl until well combined, then stir in the grated carrots. Sift in the flour, spices and baking powder, then gently fold in the dry ingredients until there are no dry spots left. Pour the batter into the lined tin, smoothing it out into the corners.

Bake: Bake the cake in the preheated oven for 35–40 minutes, until browned on top and a skewer inserted into the middle comes out clean Allow the cake to cool for several minutes in the tin before using the paper to lift it out of the tin and transferring it to a to a wire rack to cool completely.

Make the icing: Using an electric mixer, beat all the icing ingredients in a large mixing bowl for 3–5 minutes, until slightly paler and smooth.

Assemble: Make sure the cake is completely cool before cutting it into layers. Using a long, serrated bread knife, score the bottom third of the cake the whole way around. Do the same for the top third. The cake will now be scored into three layers.

Put your free hand on the top of the cake, out of the way of the knife. Slowly saw the knife back and forth along the scored line on the bottom third of the cake, cutting it all the way through to create one layer (or you can use a cheese-wire cake cutter if you have one). Do the exact same thing on the top third of the cake, keeping it straight on your scored line. The cake will now be divided into three even layers.

Gently lift up the top two layers and set them aside. Put the bottom layer on a large serving plate. Spread a little less than one-third of the cream cheese icing across the entire top of this layer. Put the middle cake layer on top of the iced bottom layer. Spread a little less than half of the remaining cream cheese icing over the top of this layer. Put the top layer on top of the iced middle layer. Coat the top and sides of the cake entirely in the rest of the cream cheese icing.

Decorate: Sprinkle the chopped walnuts around the edges on top of the cake.

Serve: Cut into 12 squares to serve.

Store: Covered in the fridge for up to three days.

Jam and custard swirl traybake

Serves 12

300g (1⅓ cups) salted butter, softened

300g (1½ cups) caster sugar

3 medium eggs

1 tsp vanilla bean paste

300g (2½ cups) self-raising flour

50g (⅓ cup) custard powder

4 tbsp whole milk

100g (¼ cup) strawberry jam

Jam and custard puddings are a favourite of mine, so when I had some spare custard waiting to be used up, I created this recipe. It's pure comfort in a cake.

Prep: Preheat the oven to 190°C (375°F). Line an 18cm x 28cm (7in x 11in) or 23cm (9in) square baking tin with non-stick baking paper, letting the paper overhang the sides so that you can use it to lift the cake out of the tin at the end.

Make the cake: Using an electric mixer, beat the butter and sugar in a medium mixing bowl for a few minutes, until pale and fluffy.

Add the eggs one at a time, beating until fully incorporated before adding the next egg. Stir in the vanilla.

Sift in the flour, then fold until there are no dry lumps left and the batter is smooth.

Make the swirl: Scoop 100g (½ cup) of the cake batter into a separate bowl, then add the custard powder and milk and stir until thoroughly combined. Pour this into a piping bag with no piping tip.

Spread the rest of the cake batter into the lined tin.

Put the jam in a separate piping bag with no tip. Cut off the tip of this piping bag, then pipe a random pattern on top of the batter. Do the same with the custard mixture.

Swirl the top of the cake with a spoon to distribute the custard and jam into the batter.

Bake: Bake the cake in the preheated oven for 35–40 minutes, until golden on top and a skewer inserted into the middle comes out clean.

Let the cake cool completely in the tin before using the paper to lift it out onto a chopping board.

Serve: Cut into 12 squares to serve.

Store: In an airtight container in the fridge for up to three days.

Red velvet traybake

Serves 12

For the cake:

240g (1 cup) buttermilk

50g (¼ cup) vegetable oil

3 medium eggs

1 tbsp red food colouring

1 tsp vanilla bean paste

150g (⅔ cup) salted butter, softened

300g (1½ cups) caster sugar

400g (3⅓ cups) plain flour

35g (heaped ¼ cup) cocoa powder

1 tsp baking soda

½ tsp baking powder

For the cream cheese icing:

200g (7oz) cream cheese

110g (½ cup) salted butter, softened

400g (3⅓ cups) icing sugar

Red velvet cake gets its name from its red colour but also because of its texture: it's an extremely soft cake that has little structural integrity. It's one of those cakes that always collapses on me at the worst possible moment. Despite being one of my favourites, I was always too afraid to bake it because it would flop, so I decided to turn it into a traybake for ease of slicing and serving without the anxiety of it becoming the Leaning Tower of Cake.

Prep: Preheat the oven to 180°C (350°F). Line an 18cm x 28cm (7in x 11in) or 23cm (9in) square baking tin with non-stick baking paper, letting the paper overhang the sides so that you can use it to lift the cake out of the tin at the end. Put one empty cupcake case on a separate small tray.

Make the cake: In a large jug, stir together the buttermilk, oil, eggs, food colouring and vanilla. Set aside.

Using an electric mixer, beat the butter and sugar in a large mixing bowl for a few minutes, until pale and fluffy.

While mixing on a low speed, pour in the liquid ingredients and continue beating until everything is just combined.

Sift in the flour, cocoa powder, baking soda and baking powder. Fold through the dry ingredients until there are no dry spots left.

Scoop out a few tablespoons of the batter and fill the cupcake case. Pour the rest of the batter into the lined tin and smooth the top.

Bake: Bake in the preheated oven for 35–40 minutes, until a skewer inserted into the middle comes out clean. Let the cake cool completely in the tin.

Bake the single cupcake on a small tray in the oven for 10–12 minutes, until a skewer inserted into the middle comes out clean. Let it cool for a few minutes, then remove it from its case.

Make the crumb: Line a small tray with non-stick baking paper (I use the tray I baked the cupcake on). Crumble the cupcake onto the tray and spread out the crumbs. Bake the cupcake crumbs on the top shelf of the oven for 5 minutes, until they are crisp and crunchy.

Make the icing: Using an electric mixer, beat the cream cheese and butter in a large mixing bowl for 5 minutes, until very pale and fluffy.

Sift in the icing sugar. On a very low speed, beat the icing sugar into the cream cheese until combined and smooth.

Assemble: When the cake is completely cool, use the paper to lift it from the tin and put it on a serving plate. Spread the cream cheese icing all over the top of the cake, then sprinkle over the cupcake crumbs.

Serve: Cut the cake into 12 squares to serve.

Store: In an airtight container in the fridge for up to three days.

Sprinkle cake with white chocolate ganache

Serves 12

For the cake:

300g (1⅓ cups) salted butter, softened

300g (1½ cups) caster sugar

3 medium eggs

1 tsp vanilla bean paste

300g (2½ cups) self-raising flour

For the white chocolate ganache:

300g (10½oz) white chocolate, cut into small pieces

120g (½ cup) double cream

To decorate:

a handful of rainbow sprinkles

This is an elevated version of the school cake that goes viral every once in a while for being so nostalgic and simple to make. Though I love royal icing, I find it's a little too sweet to spread in large quantities over a thick cake like this one. White chocolate ganache is a bit fancier and cuts through the sweetness before it gets sickly. The sprinkles are just for show but they also give the cake a little extra crunch.

Prep: Preheat the oven to 200°C (400°F). Line an 18cm x 28cm (7in x 11in) or 23cm (9in) square baking tin with non-stick baking paper, letting the paper overhang the sides so that you can use it to lift the cake out of the tin at the end.

Make the cake: Using an electric mixer, beat the butter and sugar in a large mixing bowl for a few minutes, until pale and fluffy.

Add the eggs and vanilla and beat until combined.

Sift in the flour, then fold until there are no dry lumps left and the batter is smooth.

Pour the batter into the lined tin, spreading it evenly into the corners.

Bake: Bake in the preheated oven for 35–40 minutes, until golden on top and a skewer inserted into the middle comes out clean.

Let the cake cool completely in the tin before using the paper to lift it out onto a wire rack.

Make the ganache: Put the chocolate in a medium heatproof bowl.

Pour the cream into a medium saucepan on a medium-high heat and simmer until it's just about to boil, stirring continuously so it doesn't catch on the bottom of the pan. As soon as it's about to boil, immediately take the pan off the heat and pour the hot cream over the chocolate. Let it sit for 10 minutes, then stir the cream and melted chocolate together until a smooth ganache is formed.

Spread the ganache all over the top of the cooled cake.

Decorate: Sprinkle a generous handful of rainbow sprinkles on top.

Serve: Cut into 12 squares to serve.

Store: In an airtight container in the fridge for up to three days.

Sticky toffee pudding traybake

Serves 12

300g (1¼ cups) whole milk

200g (1 scant cup) pitted dates, chopped into small chunks

1 tbsp vanilla bean paste

75g (⅓ cup) salted butter, softened

200g (1 cup) caster sugar

1 medium egg

350g (3 cups) self-raising flour

1 tsp ground cinnamon

1 tsp baking powder

For the toffee sauce:

150g (heaped ¾ cup) light brown sugar

75g (⅓ cup) salted butter

60g (¼ cup) double cream

20g (1 tbsp) golden syrup

To serve:

vanilla ice cream

The question I'm asked most often is what my favourite cake is, and now you have the answer: it's this one. Warm, gooey date cake paired with toffee sauce is my idea of paradise. Don't even try to talk to me when I'm eating this – I have either burned my mouth because I couldn't wait to eat it or I'm having a blissful moment.

Prepare the dates: Pour the milk into a medium saucepan on a high heat. Stir continuously so it doesn't catch on the bottom of the pan and remove from the heat just before it starts to boil. Stir in the chopped dates and vanilla, then set aside for 20 minutes.

Prep: Preheat the oven to 180°C (350°F). Line an 18cm x 28cm (7in x 11in) or 23cm (9in) square baking tin with non-stick baking paper.

Make the cake: Using an electric mixer, beat the butter and sugar in a large mixing bowl for a few minutes, until pale and fluffy.

Add the egg and beat again until combined.

With the mixer on a low speed, slowly pour in the warm milk and date mixture and mix until fully combined.

Sift in the flour, cinnamon and baking powder. Using a wooden spoon, fold in the dry ingredients until the batter has no visible dry sections.

Spread the batter evenly in the lined tin.

Bake: Bake in the preheated oven for 30–35 minutes, until a skewer inserted into the middle comes out clean. Keep the cake in the tin.

Make the toffee sauce: Put all the sauce ingredients in a large saucepan on a medium-low heat until fully melted. Stir continuously to prevent the sauce from catching on the bottom of the pan.

With the cake still in the tin, prick the top all over with a sharp knife, making sure you go right down to the bottom of the tin. Pour the sauce evenly across the top. I like to pour over all the sauce, but you can save some to serve on the side if you want.

Serve: You can either cut the cake into squares or scoop out portions with a large spoon. Serve with a scoop of vanilla ice cream.

Store: Covered in its tin in the fridge for up to three days.

Summery lemon and orange drizzle cake

Serves 12

350g (1½ cups) salted butter, softened

350g (1¾ cups) caster sugar

2 lemons – zest of both and juice of 1

zest of 1 large orange

3 medium eggs

200g (¾ cup + 4 tsp) whole milk

1 tsp vanilla bean paste

400g (3⅓ cups) plain flour

1 tsp baking powder

For the drizzle:

150g (¾ cup) granulated sugar

zest and juice of 1 lemon

zest and juice of 1 orange

I don't know if anyone else has this problem, but pure lemon drizzle cake is a bit too sour for me. I found a happy medium by adding oranges. The orange dials down the sourness and adds a bit of fragrance to the cake too.

Prep: Preheat the oven to 180°C (350°F). Line an 18cm x 28cm (7in x 11in) or 23cm (9in) square baking tin with non-stick baking paper, letting the paper overhang the sides so that you can use it to lift the cake out of the tin at the end.

Make the cake: Using an electric mixer, beat the butter and sugar in a large mixing bowl for a few minutes, until pale and fluffy.

Add the lemon and orange zest and beat through. Add the eggs, milk, lemon juice and vanilla and beat until combined.

Sift in the flour and baking powder and fold in until there are no dry lumps left. Pour the batter into the lined tin.

Bake: Bake in the preheated oven for 20–25 minutes, until a skewer inserted into the middle comes out clean. Leave the cake in the tin to cool completely.

Make the drizzle: In a small bowl, stir together the granulated sugar, lemon juice and orange juice until combined. Spread the drizzle on top of the cooled cake while it's still in the tin, then sprinkle the lemon and orange zest over the top of the drizzle. Allow to set for about 1 hour, until the drizzle has set with a crunch, then use the paper to lift the cake out of the tin.

Serve: Cut into 12 squares to serve.

Store: In an airtight container at room temperature for up to three days.

Tres leches cake

Serves 12

150g (1¼ cups) plain flour

1 tsp baking powder

½ tsp salt

4 medium egg yolks

100g (½ cup) caster sugar

100g (⅓ cup + 4 tsp) whole milk

1 tsp vanilla bean paste

For the egg whites:

4 medium egg whites

½ tsp cream of tartar

50g (¼ cup) caster sugar

For the soak:

1 x 410g (14oz) can of evaporated milk

1 x 397g (14oz) can of sweetened condensed milk

100g (⅓ cup + 4 tsp) whole milk

For the whipped cream:

360g (1½ cups) double cream

To decorate:

2 tbsp ground cinnamon

This cake is genuinely fun to make from start to finish. Pouring over the milks and watching them slowly soak in always feels a bit magical. It's one of those cakes you don't slice – you serve it by scooping it with a spoon.

Prep: Preheat the oven to 180°C (350°F). Get out an 18cm x 28cm (7in x 11in) or 23cm (9in) square baking tin, but do not grease or line it.

Make the cake: Sift the flour, baking powder and salt together in a mixing bowl. Set aside.

Scald a large metal bowl or the bowl of a stand mixer – do not use plastic! – with very hot water to remove any grease or residue, then dry it completely. Any grease or water would prevent a meringue from forming. Put the egg whites and cream of tartar in the bowl.

Using a spotlessly clean electric mixer or the whisk attachment of a stand mixer, whisk until soft peaks begin to form. Spoon in the 50g (¼ cup) sugar 1 tablespoon at a time, whisking for 10 seconds between each addition, until all the sugar has been incorporated into the egg whites. Beat until very stiff peaks form.

Put the egg yolks and 100g (½ cup) sugar in a separate mixing bowl. Using an electric mixer, beat for a few minutes, until pale and fluffy. When you rub the mixture between your fingertips, you shouldn't feel any graininess. Add the 100g (⅓ cup + 4 tsp) milk and vanilla and beat until combined.

Put a fine mesh sieve over the bowl with the egg yolk mixture. Sift the dry ingredients over the top, then gently fold them in, trying not to knock too much air out of the yolks.

Carefully spoon half of the egg whites into the egg yolk mixture and gently fold them together, then repeat with the remaining egg whites. Pour the batter into the ungreased tin.

Bake: Bake in the preheated oven for 20–25 minutes, until golden on top and a skewer inserted into the middle comes out clean.

For the soak: Meanwhile, combine the evaporated milk, condensed milk and whole milk in a medium bowl. Allow the cake to cool for a couple minutes in the tin before pouring over the milk mixture. Let the cake soak in the fridge for 45–60 minutes.

Whip the cream: Using an electric mixer, whisk the cream in a medium mixing bowl until it's nice and thick, being careful not to overmix the cream or it will curdle. Spread the whipped cream across the top of the soaked cake.

Decorate: Sprinkle the cinnamon across the top of the whipped cream.

Serve: Cut into 12 squares to serve.

Store: Tres leches cake is best served on the day it's made, but it can be kept covered in the fridge for up to two days.

Toasted hazelnut brownies

Makes 12

100g (¾ cup) whole, peeled hazelnuts

250g (1 cup + 2 tbsp) salted butter, cubed

200g (7oz) dark chocolate, chopped

300g (1½ cups) caster sugar

50g (5 tbsp) cocoa powder

4 medium eggs

200g (1⅔ cups) plain flour

1 tsp baking powder

For feathering the top:

50g (1¾oz) dark chocolate, chopped

Hazelnut chocolate spread is a worldwide favourite, so a brownie inspired by that flavour combo can't be wrong. Plus they look extra-fancy with the hazelnuts on top.

Prep: Preheat the oven to 180°C (350°F). Line an 18cm x 28cm (7in x 11in) or 23cm (9in) square baking tin with non-stick baking paper, letting the paper overhang the sides so that you can use it to lift the brownies out of the tin later.

Toast the hazelnuts: Put two-thirds of the hazelnuts on a small baking tray and toast them in the preheated oven for 10–12 minutes, until golden. Allow to cool, then roughly chop. Set aside. Chop the untoasted hazelnuts too and set aside in a separate bowl.

Make the brownies: Melt the butter and chocolate in a large saucepan on a medium heat, stirring constantly so it doesn't catch on the bottom. Take the saucepan off the heat, then stir in the sugar and cocoa powder. Add the eggs one at a time, beating until fully incorporated before adding the next egg.

Sift in the flour and baking powder, then stir until there are no dry lumps left. Fold in the toasted chopped hazelnuts, then pour the batter into the lined tin and smooth the top. Set aside.

Feather the top: In a small microwave-safe bowl, melt the 50g (1¾oz) dark chocolate in the microwave in 30-second increments, stirring after each one. Or you can put the chocolate in a heatproof bowl set on top of a saucepan of gently simmering water, making sure the water doesn't touch the bottom of the bowl, and melt it that way.

Let the chocolate cool for a few minutes, then pour it into a piping bag. Snip the tip off the piping bag to make as small a hole as possible, then pipe horizontal lines spaced about 1cm (½in) from each other across the top of the brownie batter. Or if you're not worried about being so precise, you could drizzle the melted chocolate over the top with a spoon instead of piping it. Using the tip of a knife, run it vertically up and down the top of the batter to create a feathered effect.

Decorate: Sprinkle the untoasted chopped hazelnuts across the top.

Bake: Bake in the preheated oven for 20–25 minutes. The centre of the brownies won't be set enough for you to test them with a skewer, so you just have to go with your gut here! The top of the brownies should be shiny and cracked and the edges should be set even though the centre will still be a little gooey.

Let the brownies cool completely in the tin, then use the baking paper to lift them out and transfer to a wire rack.

Serve: Cut into 12 squares to serve.

Store: In an airtight container at room temperature for three days.

Brookies

Makes 12

For the cookie layer:

175g (¾ cup) salted butter, softened

150g (heaped ¾ cup) light brown sugar

150g (¾ cup) caster sugar

1 medium egg

1 tsp vanilla bean paste

450g (3¾ cups) plain flour

½ tsp baking powder

½ tsp baking soda

100g (3½oz) dark chocolate, cut into chunks

For the brownie layer:

200g (¾ cup + 2 tbsp) salted butter

200g (7oz) dark chocolate

200g (1 cup) caster sugar

50g (5 tbsp) cocoa powder

2 medium eggs

100g (¾ cup) plain flour

½ tsp baking powder

Why choose between a brownie and a cookie when a brookie gives you the best of both worlds? With a crunchy cookie base and a fudgy brownie topping, they're impossible to resist.

Prep: Preheat the oven to 180°C (350°F). Line an 18cm x 28cm (7in x 11in) or 23cm (9in) square baking tin with non-stick baking paper, letting the paper overhang the sides so that you can use it to lift the brookies out at the end.

Make the cookie layer: Using an electric mixer, beat the butter and sugars in a large mixing bowl for a few minutes, until pale and fluffy.

Add the egg and vanilla and beat until combined.

Sift in the flour, baking powder and baking soda, then mix just until a dough forms. With the dough still in the bowl, knead it with your hands until almost all the flour has been combined. Add the chocolate chunks and knead until the dough is smooth and there are no dry spots.

Press the dough evenly into the base of the lined tin. Put the tin in the fridge while you make the brownie layer.

Make the brownie layer: Melt the butter and chocolate in a large saucepan on a medium heat, stirring continuously so it doesn't catch on the bottom of the pan.

Take the saucepan off the heat, then stir in the sugar and cocoa. This cools down the mixture so the eggs won't scramble when you add them.

Add the eggs one at a time, beating until fully incorporated before adding the next egg.

Sift in the flour and baking powder, then stir until there are no dry lumps left and the batter is smooth.

Assemble: Take the tin out of the fridge, then pour the brownie batter over the chilled cookie layer.

Bake: Bake in the preheated oven for 35–40 minutes, until the top of the brownies is shiny and cracked and the edges are set even though the centre will still be a little gooey.

Let the slab cool in the tin for several minutes before using the paper to lift it out onto a wire rack.

Serve: Cut into 12 squares to serve.

Store: In an airtight container at room temperature or in the fridge for extra brownie fudginess for up to five days.

Loaded blondies

200g (¾ cup + 2 tbsp) salted butter

200g (7oz) white chocolate, broken into small chunks

125g (¾ cup) light brown sugar

75g (⅓ cup) caster sugar

3 medium eggs

250g (2 cups) plain flour

70g (½ cup) coloured chocolate candies, such as Smarties or M&Ms (set a few aside to sprinkle on top)

a small handful of plain small pretzels, broken into small pieces (set aside some whole ones for the top)

Blondies are boring on their own. There, I said it. Blondies are so much better when they're packed full of fun ingredients that you find in the back of your cupboards, like the salty pretzels and candies used in these. Pure extravagance.

Prep: Preheat the oven to 180°C (350°F). Line an 18cm x 28cm (7in x 11in) or 23cm (9in) square baking tin with non-stick baking paper, letting the paper overhang the sides so that you can use it to lift the blondies out of the tin at the end.

Melt the chocolate: In a large microwave-safe bowl, melt the butter and chocolate in the microwave in 30-second increments, stirring after each one. Or you can put the butter and chocolate in a large heatproof bowl set over a saucepan of simmering water, making sure the water doesn't touch the bottom of the bowl, and melt them that way.

Stir in the sugars, then the eggs, then the flour. Finally, stir in the chocolate candies and broken pretzels.

Spread the mixture in the lined tin, making sure you get it right into the corners. Press the whole pretzels and reserved candies on top.

Bake: Bake in the preheated oven for 20-25 minutes, until the centre still has a slight a jiggle to it – it should not be fully set.

Let the blondies cool completely in the tin before using the paper to lift them out onto a chopping board.

Serve: Cut into 12 squares to serve.

Store: In an airtight container at room temperature or in the fridge for extra fudginess for up to five days.

Cinnamon and almond slices

Makes 12

200g (¾ cup + 2 tbsp) salted butter, softened

100g (½ cup) caster sugar

300g (2½ cups) plain flour

1 tsp ground cinnamon

½ tsp baking powder

1 medium egg

50g (½ cup) flaked almonds

20g (1 tbsp) granulated sugar

My granny gave me this recipe from her large folder of vintage newspaper cuttings. I have modified it slightly, but I hope you agree that these slices are worth keeping alive through the generations. I'm delighted to share my version of her recipe with you.

Prep: Preheat the oven to 180°C (350°F). Line an 18cm x 28cm (7in x 11in) or 23cm (9in) square baking tin with non-stick baking paper, letting the paper overhang the sides so that you can use it to lift the slices out of the tin at the end.

Make the dough: Using an electric mixer, beat the butter and caster sugar in a medium mixing bowl for a few minutes, until pale and fluffy.

Sift in the flour, cinnamon and baking powder. Mix just until it comes together into a dough.

Press the dough into the base of the lined tin, then flatten it with the back of a tablespoon until it's an even thickness. Prick the dough all over with a fork.

Beat the egg in a small bowl. Lightly brush the surface of the dough all over with the egg wash, then sprinkle the flaked almonds and granulated sugar on top.

Bake: Bake in the preheated oven for 20–25 minutes, until golden brown on top and the almonds are toasted.

Serve: While it's still hot and in the tin, cut into 12 squares. Allow to cool completely before using the paper to lift the squares out of the tin.

Store: In an airtight container at room temperature for up to three days.

Cinnamon sugar honey bars

110g (½ cup) salted butter

50g (2½ tbsp) runny honey

30g (1½ tbsp) caster sugar

2 medium eggs

1 tsp ground cinnamon

150g (1¼ cups) plain flour

For the topping:

100g (½ cup) granulated sugar

1 tbsp ground cinnamon

3–4 tbsp runny honey

These no-fuss bars come together quickly and slice easily into neat portions. Cinnamon and honey are two warming flavours, so I bake these bars a lot in the autumn. They are perfect with a cup of tea.

Prep: Preheat the oven to 180°C (350°F). Line an 18cm x 28cm (7in x 11in) or 23cm (9in) square baking tin with non-stick baking paper, letting the paper overhang the sides so that you can use it to lift the bars out of the tin at the end.

Make the bars: Melt the butter and honey in a large saucepan on a medium heat until liquid. Take the pan off the heat and set aside for 5 minutes to cool slightly.

Stir in the caster sugar, eggs and cinnamon until fully combined.

Add the flour and stir until there are no dry lumps in the mixture. Pour the mixture into the lined tray.

Bake: Bake in the preheated oven for 15–20 minutes, until a skewer inserted into the middle comes out clean.

Allow to cool in the tin, then use the paper to lift them out of the tin and onto a wire rack.

For the topping: Stir the granulated sugar and cinnamon together in a small bowl.

Spread the honey evenly over the top of the cake, then sprinkle the cinnamon sugar over the top.

Serve: Cut into 12 rectangular bars to serve.

Store: In an airtight container at room temperature for up to three days.

Fruity lamingtons

Makes 12

200g (¾ cup + 2 tbsp) salted butter, softened

250g (1¼ cups) caster sugar

3 medium eggs

1 tsp vanilla bean paste

250g (2 cups) self-raising flour

For the fruit coating:

200g (7oz) fresh strawberries

125g (4½oz) fresh raspberries

65g (½ cup) icing sugar

zest of 1 lemon and juice of ½

To decorate:

125g (1½ cups) desiccated coconut

When I think about Australia, I think of two things: kangaroos and lamingtons. These fruity, coconutty cakes are a brilliant way of using up berries that turned a little too mushy waiting in the fridge for you to eat them. We've all been there.

Prep: Preheat the oven to 180°C (350°F). Line an 18cm x 28cm (7in x 11in) or 23cm (9in) square baking tin with non-stick baking paper, letting the paper overhang the sides so that you can use it to lift the lamingtons out of the tin later.

Make the cake: Using an electric mixer, beat the butter and sugar in a medium mixing bowl for a few minutes, until pale and fluffy.

Add the eggs and vanilla and beat until combined.

Sift in the flour, then fold until there are no dry lumps left and the batter is smooth. Pour the batter into the lined tin, spreading it evenly into the corners.

Bake: Bake in the preheated oven for 30–35 minutes, until golden brown on top and a skewer inserted into the middle comes out clean.

Let the cake cool completely in the tin. When cool, use the paper to lift the cake from the tin, then cut into 12 squares. Set aside.

Make the fruit coating: Put a fine mesh sieve above a small bowl. Put the berries in the sieve, then use the back of a spoon to press them firmly, pushing the fruit thorough the sieve and leaving the seeds behind. Discard the seeds.

Sift the icing sugar into the bowl, then add the lemon zest and juice and whisk to combine.

Assemble: Put the desiccated coconut on a flat plate. Dip each cake square in the fruit purée, making sure you coat every side.

Roll each of the coated cake squares in the desiccated coconut, then put them on a wire rack. Allow them to dry slightly before serving.

Store: In an airtight container in the fridge for up to two days.

Millionaire's shortbread

For the shortbread layer:

275g (2¼ cups) plain flour

75g (⅓ cup) caster sugar

200g (¾ cup + 2 tbsp) salted
butter, cold and cubed

For the caramel layer:

1 x 397g (14oz) can of
condensed milk

170g (¾ cup) salted butter

60g (3 tbsp) golden syrup

30g (1½ tbsp) caster sugar

1 tsp sea salt

For the chocolate layer:

100g (3½oz) milk chocolate

100g (3½oz) dark chocolate

1 tbsp flaky sea salt

In my first job as a waitress, I brought in a few slices of my millionaire's shortbread to work and turned my back on them for two seconds, and they were all gone. Nothing can beat the buttery shortbread base, caramel filling and rich chocolate topping. Millionaire's shortbread might look like it's hard to make, but it's so simple – the key is to take your time and let each layer set fully.

Prep: Preheat the oven to 180°C (350°F). Line an 18cm x 28cm (7in x 11in) or 23cm (9in) square baking tin with non-stick baking paper, letting the paper overhang the sides so that you can use it to lift the shortbread out of the tin later.

Make the shortbread layer: Put the flour and sugar in a medium bowl and stir to combine. Add the butter, then use your fingertips to rub it into the flour until it forms a breadcrumb consistency. Tip the mixture into the lined tin, then press it firmly into the base, making sure you get it right into the corners and that it's an even thickness all over.

Bake: Bake in the preheated oven for 15–20 minutes, until the shortbread is golden around the edges.

Remove the tin from the oven. Press the shortbread all over with the back of a spoon to neaten the sides of the traybake. Set aside to cool.

Make the caramel layer: Put the condensed milk, butter, golden syrup and sugar in a large saucepan on a medium heat. Stir constantly to prevent the caramel from catching.

Once everything has dissolved, turn the heat up to high and let the caramel come to a boil. Boil for 5 minutes, stirring constantly, until it becomes slightly darker in colour and has thickened. Take the pan off the heat and stir in the salt. Pour the caramel onto the shortbread base, spreading it out evenly. Leave the caramel to set for 1 hour in a cool place until you can touch the caramel without it sticking to your finger.

Make the chocolate layer: When the caramel has set, melt the milk and dark chocolate in a medium microwave-safe bowl in 30-second intervals in the microwave, stirring after each one. Or you can put the chocolate in a heatproof bowl set on top of a saucepan of gently simmering water, making sure the water doesn't touch the bottom of the bowl, and melt it that way.

Pour the melted chocolate over the caramel, spreading it evenly into each corner. Allow the chocolate to cool and set for a few minutes, then sprinkle the flaky sea salt over the top. Chill the millionaire's shortbread in the fridge for 1 hour, until the chocolate has fully set.

Serve: Use the paper to lift the slab out of the tin, then invert it onto a clean sheet of non-stick baking paper with the chocolate side down. Score cutting lines across the shortbread base, then gently ease the knife through the layers to slice into 12 squares.

Store: In an airtight container in the fridge for up to five days.

No-bake pistachio, chocolate and caramel squares

Makes 12

250g (9oz) plain tea biscuits

110g (½ cup) salted butter

2 x 40g (1½oz) chocolate caramel bars

20g (1 tbsp) golden syrup

20g (1 tbsp) caster sugar

30g (¼ cup) chopped pistachios

For the topping:

300g (10½oz) milk chocolate, broken into pieces

30g (¼ cup) chopped pistachios

This recipe (without the pistachio) was handwritten by my late great-grandma. She was the first woman I knew of in my family who enjoyed baking as much as I do. My mum told me that when she'd go home for a visit from university, her grandmother would make a batch that she'd bring back to her dorm room to share with her friends. I can see why they loved these – I ate half of the batch all on my own while testing the recipe!

Prep: Line an 18cm x 28cm (7in x 11in) or 23cm (9in) square baking tin with non-stick baking paper, letting the paper overhang the sides so that you can use it to lift the slab out of the tin at the end.

Make the biscuit base: Put the biscuits in a food processor and blitz until they're all crushed to a fine powder. Alternatively, you could put them in a large ziplock bag and bash them with a rolling pin. Set aside.

Put the butter, chocolate caramel bars, golden syrup and sugar in a large saucepan on a low heat, stirring until everything has melted together into a liquid.

Add the chopped pistachios and crushed biscuits. Stir until completely combined.

Tip the mixture into the lined tin. Press it down evenly, making sure you get it into the corners. Set aside.

Make the topping: In a small microwave-safe bowl, melt the chocolate in the microwave in 30-second increments, stirring after each one. Or you can put the chocolate in a heatproof bowl set on top of a saucepan of gently simmering water, making sure the water doesn't touch the bottom of the bowl, and melt it that way.

Assemble: Pour the melted chocolate on top of the biscuit base in the tin, spreading it out evenly to each corner. Sprinkle the chopped pistachios over the top.

Freeze: Chill the tin in the freezer for 1 hour, until the bars are fully set.

Serve: Use the paper to lift the slab out of the tin. Using a sharp knife, cut into 12 squares to serve.

Store: In an airtight container in the fridge for up to three days but bring to room temperature before eating.

Chocolate-dipped oat and raisin bars

Makes 12

75g (⅓ cup) salted butter

50g (heaped ¼ cup) light brown sugar

20g (1 tbsp) golden syrup

250g (3¼ cups) porridge oats

50g (scant ½ cup) plain flour

100g (⅔ cup) raisins

To decorate:

100g (3½oz) dark chocolate, broken into pieces

The issue I have with oat bars is that as soon as I put one in my lunchbox, it turns to dust when so much as gently pressed. The solution? Dipping the bars in chocolate prevents them from crumbling. Or maybe I just needed to add chocolate to my oat bars because I like chocolate. No judgement! Instead of raisins, try using chocolate chips or chopped hazelnuts.

Prep: Preheat the oven to 190°C (375°F). Line an 18cm x 28cm (7in x 11in) or 23cm (9in) square baking tin with non-stick baking paper, letting the paper overhang the sides so that you can use it to lift the bars out of the tin at the end.

Make the bars: Put the butter, brown sugar and golden syrup in a large saucepan on a low heat and melt them together until they're all liquid.

Add the oats and flour. Stir until there is no visible flour left and all the oats are evenly covered in the melted mixture. Add the raisins and stir them through.

Pour the oat mixture into the lined tin, pressing it into each corner and making sure it's an even thickness.

Bake: Bake in the preheated oven for 18–20 minutes, until golden brown and crisp on top.

Leave to cool in the tin, then use the paper to lift the slab out of the tin and cut into 12 rectangular bars.

Decorate: Spread out a large sheet of non-stick baking paper on a flat surface.

In a small microwave-safe bowl, melt the chocolate in the microwave in 30-second increments, stirring after each one. Or you can put the chocolate in a heatproof bowl set on top of a saucepan of gently simmering water, making sure the water doesn't touch the bottom of the bowl, and melt it that way.

Working with one cooled oat bar at a time and holding it horizontally, dip it into the melted chocolate until the bottom is covered. Let any excess chocolate drip off while holding the bar over the bowl.

Put the dipped oat bar on the sheet of non-stick baking paper and allow to set completely before serving.

Store: In an airtight container in the fridge for up to five days.

CAKES, CUPCAKES & MUFFINS

Classic baked cheesecake

Serves 8

300g (1½ cups) caster sugar

5 medium eggs

900g (2lb) cream cheese

250g (1 cup) double cream

50g (scant ½ cup) plain flour

To serve:

fresh berries

I have never seen such disappointment on my dad's face than when he cut into my baked cheesecake and realised there was no biscuit base. Sorry, Dad! Unfortunately for him, I love making baked cheesecake and the lack of a base doesn't bother me. And no, Dad, it is heavily caramelised, not burnt.

Prep: Preheat the oven to 220°C (430°F). Line a 20cm (8in) springform cake tin with non-stick baking paper. Put this on a lined baking tray to catch any leaks while baking.

Make the cheesecake: Using an electric mixer, beat the sugar and eggs in a large mixing bowl for 3–5 minutes, until pale.

Add the cream cheese, double cream and flour. Beat until smooth and there are no dry flour lumps left in the batter. Pour the batter into the lined tin, then flatten the top with a spoon.

Bake: Bake in the preheated oven for 25 minutes, then turn the temperature down to 180°C (350°F) and bake for 20-25 minutes more. The top should be a rich caramel brown colour and the centre of the cheesecake should still have a slight jiggle to it.

Allow the cheesecake to cool completely in the tin, then run a knife or offset spatula around the edges of the tin before releasing the sides. Transfer it to the fridge for 1–2 hours to set fully.

Serve: Cut into eight slices and serve with fresh berries on the side.

Store: Covered in the fridge for up to three days.

No-bake lemon curd cheesecake

Serves 8

250g (9oz) plain tea biscuits

75g (⅓ cup) salted butter, melted

600g (1lb 5oz) cream cheese

250g (1 cup) double cream

zest and juice of 1 lemon

For the lemon curd:

50g (¼ cup) caster sugar

15g (1½ tbsp) cornflour

1 medium egg yolk

zest and juice of 1 lemon

When I want a crowd-pleasing dessert, this cheesecake is what I make. It's quick to put together, then you can pop it in the fridge the night before you want to serve it. Or if you want a solid cheesecake master recipe to add your own flavour variations to, just leave out the lemon.

Prep: Line the base and sides of a 23cm (9in) springform cake tin with non-stick baking paper.

Make the biscuit base: Put the biscuits in a food processor and blitz to a fine powder (or put them in a medium bowl and bash them with a rolling pin). Stir in the melted butter until completely combined. Tip the biscuit mixture into the lined tin and press it down firmly until there are no gaps. Set aside.

Make the cheesecake: Using an electric mixer, beat the cream cheese, double cream and lemon zest and juice in a large mixing bowl for a few minutes, until smooth and thickened slightly. Pour the cream cheese mixture on top of the biscuit base in the tin and smooth it out until it's completely flat on top.

Chill the cheesecake in the fridge for at least 2 hours to allow it to set.

Make the curd: Meanwhile, put all the ingredients for the curd in a small saucepan on a medium-high heat, stirring constantly until smooth and it comes to a boil. Remove the pan from the heat and allow to cool.

Assemble: When the curd is cool, spread it over the top of the set cheesecake. Return to the fridge for another 3–4 hours to allow the cheesecake to set fully.

Serve: When the cheesecake has set, run a knife or offset spatula around the edges of the tin before releasing the sides, then transfer the cake to a serving plate. Cut into eight slices to serve.

Store: Covered in the fridge for up to three days.

Chocolate orange marmorkuchen

Makes 1 loaf

225g (1 cup) salted butter, softened

250g (1¼ cups) caster sugar

3 medium eggs

80g (⅓ cup) milk

1 tsp vanilla bean paste

325g (2¾ cups) plain flour

2 tsp baking powder

50g (5 tbsp) cocoa powder

zest and juice of 1 large orange

For the icing:

100g (¾ cup) icing sugar

75g (⅓ cup) salted butter, softened

30g (¼ cup) cocoa powder

Marmorkuchen ('marble cake') is one of my favourite desserts, and the combo of orange and chocolate is up there too, so for me this is the ultimate cake. While I was developing this recipe, I dropped the first cake on the floor. It's the only time I've seen my brother genuinely sad about not being able to eat one of my baked goods.

Prep: Preheat the oven to 190°C (375°F). Line a 900g (2lb) loaf tin with non-stick baking paper.

Make the cake: Using an electric mixer, beat the butter and sugar in a large mixing bowl for a few minutes, until pale and fluffy.

Add the eggs, milk and vanilla and beat until combined.

Sift in the flour and baking powder. Using a wooden spoon, fold in just until there are no dry lumps left and the batter is smooth.

Transfer half of the batter to a separate bowl. Sift in the cocoa powder and mix just until thoroughly combined. Set aside.

Add two-thirds of the orange zest to the plain vanilla cake batter and stir until just combined. Set the rest aside for decoration.

Pour 3 tablespoons of the orange juice (depending on your orange, you will have approximately this amount) into the vanilla batter and mix until smooth.

Put 1 tablespoon of the vanilla and orange batter in the bottom of the lined loaf tin. Add 1 tablespoon of the chocolate batter right beside it. Repeat, alternating the vanilla and chocolate cake batter for a marbled effect, until all the batter has been used.

Bake: Bake in the preheated oven for 45–50 minutes, until a skewer inserted into the middle comes out clean. Leave to cool completely in the tin.

Make the icing: Sift the icing sugar into a mixing bowl, then add the butter. Using an electric mixer, beat for a few minutes, until pale and fluffy. Sift in the cocoa powder and beat for another minute, until fully incorporated and smooth.

Remove the loaf cake from the tin. Spread the icing all over the top, then sprinkle with the reserved orange zest.

Serve: Cut into slices to reveal the marbled effect.

Store: In an airtight container at room temperature for up to three days.

Pear loaf cake

2 large pears, peeled

200g (¾ cup + 2 tbsp) salted butter, softened

200g (1 cup) caster sugar

2 medium eggs

1 tsp vanilla bean paste

225g (1¾ cups) self-raising flour

To decorate (optional):

icing sugar

To serve (optional):

crème fraîche

I love baking with pear – it melts in the mouth and caramelises beautifully. A slice of this loaf cake is perfect with a cup of tea.

Prep: Preheat the oven to 180°C (350°F). Line a 900g (2lb) loaf tin with non-stick baking paper.

Using a sharp knife, cut the pears in half and remove the cores. Slice each half into thin, vertical slices, but keep the slices attached at the top so that you can spread them out slightly in a fan. Set aside.

Make the cake: Using an electric mixer, beat the butter and sugar in a large mixing bowl for a few minutes, until pale and fluffy.

Add the eggs and vanilla and beat until combined.

Sift in the flour, then fold until there are no dry lumps left and the batter is smooth.

Pour the batter into the lined loaf tin, then add the fanned-out pear halves on top, pressing them down slightly. They will sink into the cake as it bakes.

Bake: Bake in the preheated oven for about 1 hour, until the loaf is golden on top and a skewer inserted into the middle comes out clean.

Allow the cake to cool in the tin for at least 30 minutes before removing and allowing to cool completely on a wire rack.

Decorate: When the cake has completely cooled, dust it with icing sugar (if using).

Serve: Cut into thick slices and serve with a dollop of crème fraîche, if you like.

Store: In an airtight container at room temperature for up to two days.

Sticky ginger loaf

200g (¾ cup + 2 tbsp) salted butter

150g (½ cup) golden syrup

50g (3 tbsp) treacle

1 medium egg

150g (½ cup + 2 tbsp) buttermilk

2 tbsp ground ginger

½ tsp ground nutmeg

350g (3 cups) self-raising flour

For the glaze:

80g (4 tbsp) golden syrup

30g (2 tbsp) water

To serve:

warm custard (page 182)

If you gave me a thick slice of this cake with a dollop of custard, there is a 100% chance I would fall in love with you. Too much? Probably. But that's how much I love this cake. It's all about warmth and deep, spicy flavour.

Prep: Preheat the oven to 180°C (350°F). Line a 900g (2lb) loaf tin with non-stick baking paper.

Put the butter, golden syrup and treacle in a large saucepan on a medium heat and let them melt together. Take the pan off the heat and allow to cool for a few minutes.

Whisk the egg, buttermilk and spices together in a jug. Slowly pour the buttermilk mixture into the melted butter while stirring vigorously.

Sift in the flour, then fold until there are no dry lumps left and the batter is smooth. Pour the batter into the lined loaf tin.

Bake: Bake in the preheated oven for about 1 hour, until a skewer inserted into the middle comes out clean. If the top of the cake is getting too dark and it hasn't fully baked through, cover the top of the cake with foil and continue baking.

Make the glaze: While the cake is baking, put the golden syrup and water in a small saucepan on a high heat to melt them together. Stir continuously until it just reaches a boil, then take the pan off the heat and allow to cool.

When the cake has fully baked and is still hot, use a sharp knife to prick some holes in the top down to the centre of the cake. Pour the glaze over the top of the cake, then leave the cake to cool completely in the tin.

Serve: Cut into thick slices and serve with a generous helping of warm custard.

Store: In an airtight container at room temperature for up to three days.

White chocolate, lime curd and raspberry loaf

Makes 1 loaf

225g (1 cup) salted butter, softened

225g (heaped 1 cup) caster sugar

3 medium eggs

zest of 1 lime

1 tsp vanilla bean paste

250g (2 cups) self-raising flour, plus extra for dusting

100g (3½oz) fresh or frozen raspberries (thawed and patted dry if frozen)

100g (½ cup) white chocolate chips

For the lime curd:

50g (¼ cup) caster sugar

1 medium egg yolk

zest and juice of 1 lime

½ tsp lime-green food colouring (optional)

For the lime buttercream:

200g (1⅔ cups) icing sugar

75g (⅓ cup) salted butter, softened

zest and juice of 2 limes (about 4 tbsp juice)

To decorate:

a handful of fresh raspberries

50g (1¾oz) white chocolate, cut into chunks

This recipe came about when I wanted a cake that wasn't too rich or indulgent. The lime cuts through the sweetness, the raspberries add a bit of freshness and the chocolate, well, is chocolate!

Make the lime curd: Put the caster sugar, egg yolk and lime zest and juice in a small saucepan on a medium-high heat and bring to a boil, stirring constantly until smooth. Remove the pan from the heat and allow to cool before stirring in the food colouring (if using). Set aside while you make the cake to let the curd cool completely (or you could make the curd the day before and keep it in the fridge, but no longer as it starts to brown after a day).

Prep: Preheat the oven to 190°C (375°F). Line a 900g (2lb) loaf tin with non-stick baking paper.

Make the cake: Using an electric mixer, beat the butter and sugar in a large mixing bowl for a few minutes, until pale and fluffy.

Add the eggs, lime zest and vanilla and beat until combined.

Sift in the flour, then fold until there are no dry lumps left and the batter is smooth.

Put the raspberries in a bowl and toss with approx. 3 tablespoons of self-raising flour to prevent them from sinking to the bottom of the cake. Add the flour-dusted raspberries and the white chocolate chips to the batter and fold to combine. Spoon the batter into the lined tin and smooth the top.

Bake: Bake in the oven for 35–40 minutes, until golden on top and a skewer inserted into the middle comes out clean.

Let the loaf cool in the tin for a few minutes before removing it to a wire rack to cool completely.

Make the lime buttercream: Using an electric mixer, beat the icing sugar, butter, half of the lime zest and all of the juice in a medium mixing bowl for 5–8 minutes, until pale and there is no graininess. If the buttercream is too thick, add 1 tablespoon of water at a time and beat until looser.

Spread the buttercream on top of the cooled loaf cake. Spoon the lime curd over the top of the buttercream, then gently swirl it through.

Decorate: Press a handful of fresh raspberries and white chocolate chunks on top of the buttercream, then sprinkle over the remaining lime zest.

Serve: Cut into thick slices to serve.

Store: In an airtight container in the fridge for up to three days, though the curd will start to brown after one day.

Chocolate cherry cake

Serves 8

850g (4¼ cups) caster sugar

200g (¾ cup + 4 tsp) vegetable oil

1 tsp vanilla bean paste

450g (1¾ cups + 2 tbsp) buttermilk

4 medium eggs

1kg (8½ cups) plain flour

120g (1 cup) cocoa powder

2 tsp baking powder

2 tsp baking soda

1 tsp salt

For the syrup and filling:

100g (½ cup) caster sugar

100g (⅓ cup + 4 tsp) water

1 x 420g (14¾oz) can of pitted black cherries in syrup

50g (¼ cup) kirsch (optional)

For the cream:

100g (¾ cup) icing sugar

700g (approx. 3 cups) double cream

To decorate:

200g (7oz) dark chocolate, grated

30g (1½ tbsp) granulated sugar

8 fresh cherries with stems

I'm not a big fan of the traditional Black Forest gateau, so this is my take on the famous dessert. Chocolate and cherry are a match made in heaven, but in a cake covered in cream and chocolate shavings too? Now that's a proper showstopper.

Prep: Preheat the oven to 190°C (375°F). Line three 20cm (8in) cake tins with non-stick baking paper.

Make the cake: Using an electric mixer, whisk the sugar, oil and vanilla in a large mixing bowl until well combined. Add the buttermilk and eggs and mix until just combined.

Sift in the flour, cocoa powder, baking powder, baking soda and salt. Fold until no flour is visible and the batter is smooth.

Divide the batter evenly among the three lined tins and smooth the tops.

Bake: Bake in the preheated oven for 35–40 minutes, until a skewer inserted into the middle of the cakes comes out clean.

Let the cakes cool in the tins for a few minutes, then turn them out and transfer to a wire rack to cool completely.

Make the syrup: Put the sugar and water in a medium saucepan on a high heat and bring to a boil. Remove the pan from the heat and set aside to let the syrup cool.

Once cool, pour in the syrup from the can of pitted cherries and the kirsch (if using) and stir to combine.

When the cakes are cool, reserve a small amount of the syrup to dip the cherries in later. Divide the rest of the syrup into thirds, then pour one-third over each cake. Use a pastry brush to spread it evenly over each cake. The cakes are now ready to stack.

Whip the cream: Sift the icing sugar into a medium mixing bowl and pour in the cream. Using an electric mixer, whisk together until softly whipped, being careful not to overmix the cream or it will curdle. Store the whipped cream in the fridge until you're ready to stack the cakes if you want to do this ahead of time.

Assemble: Put a small dollop of whipped cream in the middle of your serving plate or cake stand, then put the first syrup-soaked cake on top of this dollop. Using a spoon, spread a thick layer of whipped cream on top of the cake. Make a shallow well in the middle.

Put one-third of the canned cherries in the well, distributing them uniformly in the centre.

Put the second cake on top. Repeat with another thick layer of whipped cream on top and one-third of the canned cherries in the middle.

Add the final cake layer. Using an offset spatula, spread a thin layer of whipped cream all over the top and sides, making sure the entire cake is covered.

Decorate: Press handfuls of the grated chocolate onto the sides and top of the cake until it's covered all over.

Put the final bit of whipped cream in a piping bag with a star-shaped nozzle, then pipe eight swirls on top of the cake.

Add the remaining canned cherries in a pile in the middle of the top cake layer.

Put the granulated sugar in a small bowl. Working with one fresh cherry at a time, dip each one into the leftover syrup, then into the sugar, making sure each one is completely coated. Nestle a sugared cherry on top of each swirl of whipped cream.

Serve: Cut into eight slices to serve.

Store: Covered in the fridge for up to two days.

Chocolate fudge cake

Serves 8

200g (7oz) dark chocolate, broken into small pieces

150g (⅔ cup) salted butter, softened

200g (1 cup) caster sugar

160g (⅔ cup) buttermilk

50g (¼ cup) vegetable oil

3 medium eggs

1 tsp vanilla bean paste

250g (2 cups) plain flour

75g (⅔ cup) cocoa powder

1 tsp baking powder

1 tsp baking soda

For the ganache:

300g (10½oz) dark chocolate, broken into small pieces

300g (1¼ cups) double cream

To serve (optional):

crème fraîche

This is the cake I bake when just a 'bit' of chocolate simply won't do. It's rich, dense and unapologetically indulgent.

Prep: Preheat the oven to 190°C (375°F). Line two 20cm (8in) cake tins with non-stick baking paper.

Make the cake: In a small microwave-safe bowl, melt the chocolate in the microwave in 30-second increments, stirring after each one. Or you can put the chocolate in a heatproof bowl set on top of a saucepan of gently simmering water, making sure the water doesn't touch the bottom of the bowl, and melt it that way. Let it cool slightly.

Using an electric mixer, beat the butter and sugar in a large mixing bowl for a few minutes, until pale and fluffy.

Beat in the buttermilk, oil, eggs and vanilla until combined, then stir in the melted chocolate.

Sift in the flour, cocoa powder, baking powder and baking soda. Fold through until there are no dry lumps left and the batter is smooth. Divide the batter evenly between the lined cake tins.

Bake: Bake in the preheated oven for 25–30 minutes, until a skewer inserted into the middle of each cake comes out clean.

Let the cakes cool in their tins, then turn them out onto a wire rack to cool completely before icing.

Make the ganache: Put the chocolate in a large heatproof bowl.

Pour the cream into a medium saucepan on a medium-high heat and simmer until it's just about to boil, stirring continuously so it doesn't catch on the bottom of the pan. As soon as it's about to boil, immediately take the pan off the heat and pour the hot cream over the chocolate. Let it sit for 10 minutes, then stir the cream and melted chocolate together until a smooth ganache is formed. Let the ganache cool in the fridge for 45 minutes to firm up before use. (If you accidentally let it get too firm, just leave it out at room temperature for 30 minutes, then stir to loosen it again.)

Assemble: Put one of the cakes on a serving plate, bottom side up.

Using a small offset spatula, spread a thick layer of ganache on top of this cake layer. Put the other cake on top of the ganache, bottom side up.

Cover the top and sides of the cake with the rest of the ganache, then smooth the top.

Serve: Cut into eight slices to serve, with a dollop of crème fraîche on top if you like.

Store: Covered in the fridge for up to three days.

Raspberry and almond Battenberg cake

Serves 8–10

200g (¾ cup + 2 tbsp) salted butter, softened

200g (1 cup) caster sugar

3 medium eggs

50g (½ cup) ground almonds

1 tsp vanilla bean paste

300g (2½ cups) self-raising flour

1 heaped tbsp freeze-dried raspberry powder

1 tsp pink or red food colouring

To assemble:

125g (½ cup) seedless raspberry jam

500g (1lb 2oz) marzipan

3 heaped tbsp apricot jam, melted until liquid

Battenberg cake looks intimidating, but building the layers and revealing that signature chequered pattern when you cut a slice is half the fun! Get your ruler out, though, as you do need to measure precisely for this cake.

Prep: Preheat the oven to 190°C (375°F). Line an 18cm x 28cm (7in x 11in) baking tin with non-stick baking paper, letting the paper overhang the sides so that you can use it to lift the cake out of the tin at the end. Fold a long piece of foil so that it's the same height and length as the tin. Put the foil barrier in the tin, splitting it down the middle lengthways so that the tin is divided into two halves.

Make the cake: Using an electric mixer, beat the butter and sugar in a large mixing bowl for a few minutes, until pale and fluffy. Add the eggs one at a time, beating until fully incorporated before adding the next egg. Stir in the ground almonds and vanilla.

Sift in the flour, then fold until there are no dry lumps left and the batter is smooth. Pour half of the batter into one side of the tin. Smooth the top.

Add the freeze-dried raspberry powder and food colouring to the remaining half of the batter, stirring until smooth and evenly coloured. Pour the raspberry batter into the opposite side of the tin. Smooth the top.

Bake: Bake in the preheated oven for 20–25 minutes, until golden on top and a skewer inserted into the middle comes out clean.

Let the cake cool in the tin for several minutes before removing the two halves from the tin and transferring them to a wire rack to cool completely.

Assemble: Cut the vanilla cake lengthways into two strips that are each 2.5cm (1in) wide. (There will be offcuts.) Repeat with the raspberry cake.

Put one strip of vanilla cake on a serving plate. Spread the inside edge of the cake with raspberry jam. Put one strip of raspberry cake beside the jammy edge of the vanilla cake on the serving plate, then stick the inner sides together. Spread the top of both strips with jam.

Put the other strip of vanilla cake on top of the raspberry cake. Spread the inside edge of the vanilla cake with jam. Put the second strip of raspberry cake on top of the vanilla cake so that you now have a 2x2 checkerboard of cake if you look at it from the side. Stick the inner sides together.

Tear off a large sheet of non-stick baking paper, then put the marzipan on the paper. Roll it out until it's a rectangle that fits the complete length of the cake and is four times wider than the cake (approximately 18cm x 20cm (7in x 8in)).

Carefully lift the assembled cake from the serving plate and put it in the middle of the rolled marzipan. Using a pastry brush, spread the melted apricot jam all over the top and sides of the cake.

Using the baking paper to help you, gently encourage the marzipan up the sides of the cake and over the top so that it's completely encased.

Move the cake back to the serving plate, making sure the seam of marzipan is on the bottom. Peel off the baking paper, then slice away any excess marzipan with a sharp knife.

Serve: Cut into 8–10 slices.

Store: In an airtight container at room temperature for three days.

Raspberry ripple Swiss roll

125g (heaped ½ cup) caster sugar

4 medium eggs

1 tsp vanilla bean paste

150g (1¼ cups) self-raising flour

2 tbsp freeze-dried raspberry powder

1 tsp red food colouring

For the filling:

100g (⅔ cup) raspberry jam

100g (⅓ cup + 4 tsp) double cream

100g (3½oz) fresh raspberries

This is one of those bakes that looks far more impressive than it actually is, which is exactly why I make it so often. Slicing into it and seeing that beautiful swirl never gets old. Nothing about a Swiss roll needs to be overthought – it truly is so simple.

Prep: Preheat the oven to 180°C (350°F). Line a Swiss roll tin with non-stick baking paper.

Make the cake: Using an electric mixer, whisk the sugar and eggs in a large mixing bowl for about 5 minutes, until very light and frothy.

Add the vanilla and whisk to combine.

Sift in the flour and gently fold until there are no dry lumps left and the batter is smooth.

Pour two-thirds of the batter onto the lined tin, spreading it evenly into the corners.

Sift the raspberry powder on top of the batter that's left in the bowl, then fold it through until combined. Stir in the red food colouring.

Dollop the raspberry batter on top of the plain batter in the tin, then swirl it through to create a marbled effect.

Bake: Bake in the preheated oven for 10–12 minutes, until the top is golden and a skewer inserted into the middle comes out clean.

Form the roll: Put a large sheet of non-stick baking paper on a clean work surface. As soon as the cake comes out of the oven, flip it out onto the paper, being careful not to break it.

Starting with the long edge furthest from you and using the baking paper to help you, roll the cake tightly towards yourself into a roll. Let the cake cool completely in this rolled position, leaving the baking paper in place.

When the cake is cool, carefully unroll it and remove the paper. Spread out a new sheet of baking paper, then transfer the cake on top of this sheet.

Make the filling: Spread the jam all over the top of the Swiss roll.

Using an electric mixer, whisk the cream in a medium mixing bowl until it's nice and thick, being careful not to overmix the cream or it will curdle. Spread the whipped cream on top of the jam, leaving a small edge clear on the long edge where the roll will end.

Scatter over the raspberries, then push them into the cream. Using the paper to help you, roll up the cake to enclose the filling, rolling it towards the long edge of the roll where you left a small edge clear of whipped cream.

Serve: Put on a serving plate, seam side down. Cut into eight slices to serve.

Store: In an airtight container in the fridge for up to two days.

Tarta de Santiago

Serves 8

300g (3 cups) almond flour
(see the intro)

100g (½ cup) caster sugar

100g (1 cup) flaked almonds

4 medium eggs

zest of 1 lemon

1 tsp ground cinnamon

To decorate:

icing sugar, to dust

To serve:

whipped cream

sliced fresh strawberries
(optional)

Tarta de Santiago is a traditional Galician almond cake associated with the pilgrimage city of Santiago de Compostela, where the Camino ends. The cake is finished with the cross of St James stencilled in icing sugar on top, a symbol of St James the Apostle and the Camino. You can buy these stencils if you make this cake a lot (and I do!) or you can download a template online and print it. This cake was brought to me as a gift from a Spanish friend, and I haven't stopped baking it ever since.

Almond flour is similar to ground almonds but it's milled a lot more finely. If you can't find almond flour, you can just blitz the same amount of ground almonds in a food processor or blender to make them finer.

Prep: Preheat the oven to 180°C (350°F). Line a 20cm (8in) springform cake tin with non-stick baking paper.

Make the cake: Put all the cake ingredients in a medium bowl. Using a spatula, stir together into a smooth, thick batter.

Pour the batter into the lined tin, pressing it into the edges.

Bake: Bake in the preheated oven for 35–40 minutes, until the cake is golden on top and a skewer inserted into the middle comes out clean.

Leave the cake to cool in the tin completely before releasing it from the tin and transferring to a serving plate.

Decorate: While the cake is cooling, cut a piece of baking paper into the shape of the cross of St James. (There are lots of templates online for the cross.) Put the cross cut-out on the centre of the cooled cake. Using a small sieve, dust the top of the cake completely with icing sugar.

Gently remove the template from the top of the cake to reveal the cross.

Serve: My favourite way to serve a slice of this cake is with a dollop of whipped cream and a few sliced strawberries, if you like.

Store: In an airtight container at room temperature for up to three days.

Tarta San Marcos

Serves 10

340g (1½ cups) salted butter, softened

340g (1¾ cups) caster sugar

5 medium eggs

1 tbsp vanilla bean paste

340g (2¾ cups) self-raising flour

For the syrup:

100g (½ cup) caster sugar

100g (⅓ cup + 4 tsp) water

20g (4 tsp) rum

For the custard topping:

75g (⅓ cup) caster sugar

1 medium egg yolk

20g (4 tsp) water

10g (1 tbsp) cornflour

For the filling:

750g (3 cups + 2 tbsp) double cream

1 tsp vanilla bean paste

20g (2 tbsp) cocoa powder

To decorate:

150g (1½ cups) flaked almonds

2 tbsp caster sugar

Tarta San Marcos is a showstopping cake. The flavours are a little hard to describe, but think caramelised custard, rum-soaked vanilla genoise sponge, chocolate cream and toasted almonds. It dates to the 12th century, when it was created as a tribute to Infanta Sancha Raimúndez of León following her visit to the Convent of San Marcos in León. Her contributions helped fund the convent, which was dedicated to caring for pilgrims travelling the French Way to Santiago who rested in León.

Prep: Preheat the oven to 190°C (375°F). Line three 20cm (8in) cake tins with non-stick baking paper.

Make the syrup: Put the sugar and water in a small saucepan on a high heat to dissolve the sugar. When the syrup starts to boil, take the pan off the heat and allow to cool, then stir in the rum and set aside.

Make the custard: Put the sugar, egg yolk, water and cornflour in a medium saucepan and whisk together. Put the saucepan on a low heat initially until the custard begins to warm up, then slowly increase the heat while stirring constantly. As soon as the custard starts to bubble and boil, remove the pan from the heat. Keep stirring for a few minutes after taking it off the heat as the bottom can still catch! Set the custard aside until it's cool and the cake is ready to decorate.

Make the cake: Using an electric mixer, beat the butter and sugar in a large mixing bowl for a few minutes, until pale and fluffy.

Add the eggs one at a time, beating until fully incorporated before adding the next egg. Stir in the vanilla.

Sift in the flour, then fold until there are no dry lumps left and the batter is smooth. Divide the batter evenly among the three lined tins.

Bake: Bake in the preheated oven for 15–20 minutes, until a skewer inserted into the middle of each cake comes out clean.

Leave the cakes to cool fully in their tins while you make the filling.

Make the filling: Put the cream and vanilla in a large mixing bowl. Using an electric mixer, whisk until medium peaks form.

Put one-third of the whipped cream in a separate bowl and whisk in the cocoa powder.

Put another third of the whipped cream into a piping bag with a star tip.

Assemble: Turn the cooled cakes out of their tins. Using a pastry brush, spread the syrup across the top of each cake until they are thoroughly soaked.

Put a small dollop of whipped cream on the middle of a serving plate to hold the cake in place. Put the first cake layer on top of this dollop, then spread the vanilla cream that's left in the bowl across the top.

Put another cake layer on top of the vanilla cream. Spread the chocolate cream evenly across the top of this layer. Add the final cake layer.

Decorate: Using most of the whipped cream in the piping bag, spread a thin layer across the sides of the cake, then press the flaked almonds against it.

Pour the custard on top of the cake in a thin layer, making sure it does not drip down the sides.

Sprinkle the custard topping with the 2 tablespoons of sugar.

Using a culinary blow torch, torch the custard until it turns a deep golden brown. Pipe a border of whipped cream on top of the cake to hold it in.

Serve: Cut into 10 slices to serve.

Store: Covered in the fridge for up to three days.

Tiramisu cake

Serves 8

500g (2½ cups) caster sugar

130g (½ cup + 1 tbsp) vegetable oil

1 tsp vanilla bean paste

350g (1½ cups) buttermilk

3 medium eggs

700g (5¾ cups) plain flour

2 tsp baking powder

2 tsp baking soda

1 tsp salt

60g (½ cup) cocoa powder

For the mascarpone icing:

300g (1⅓ cups) salted butter, softened

900g (7½ cups) icing sugar

200g (7oz) mascarpone

For the coffee soak:

10g (2 tbsp) instant coffee granules

150g (½ cup + 2 tbsp) boiling water

For the filling:

6 ladyfingers, plus extra to decorate

To decorate (optional):

1 tbsp cocoa powder

Tiramisu is arguably the most popular dessert on any menu, so why not make it into a cake? It has all the hallmark flavours of coffee, cream and cocoa, but turned into an eye-catching centrepiece.

Prep: Preheat the oven to 190°C (375°F). Line three 20cm (8in) cake tins with non-stick baking paper.

Make the cake: Using an electric mixer, beat the sugar, oil and vanilla in a large mixing bowl until combined.

Add one-third of the buttermilk and one egg, then beat until combined. Do this twice more, until all the buttermilk and eggs have been added.

Sift in the flour, baking powder, baking soda and salt. Fold in until there are no dry lumps left and the batter is smooth.

Scoop one-third of the batter into a separate bowl. Add the cocoa powder and stir to combine, then pour the chocolate batter into one of the lined tins.

Divide the plain batter evenly between the other two lined tins.

Bake: Bake in the preheated oven for 15–20 minutes, until a skewer inserted into the middle of each cake comes out clean. Let the cakes cool in the tins for 10 minutes before turning out and transferring to wire racks to cool completely.

Cut each cake in half horizontally with a serrated bread knife or a wire cake cutter. You will have four vanilla layers and two chocolate layers.

Make the mascarpone icing: Using an electric mixer, beat the butter in a medium mixing bowl for 10 minutes, until it's very pale. Sift in the icing sugar and beat for another 3 minutes, then add the mascarpone and beat until fully combined.

Make the coffee soak: Put the instant coffee in a small heatproof bowl, then pour over the boiling water, stirring until the coffee has dissolved. Using a pastry brush, spread the coffee across the top of each cake layer until they are all thoroughly soaked.

Make the filling: In a small bowl, crush the ladyfingers into large chunks.

Assemble: Put a small dollop of mascarpone icing in the middle of your serving plate to hold the cake in place, then put the first vanilla cake layer on top of that dollop. Spread some of the mascarpone icing on top of that cake layer, then add a sprinkling of the crushed ladyfingers.

Put a chocolate cake layer on top of this, then spread that with mascarpone icing and crushed ladyfingers too.

Do the same with two more vanilla layers, then a chocolate layer, then the final vanilla layer. Do not put any crushed ladyfingers on the final layer, as this is the top of the cake.

Spread the entire outside of the cake with a thin layer of the mascarpone icing. Put the rest of the icing in a piping bag with a star nozzle, then pipe eight swirls evenly spaced around the top outside edge of the cake.

Decorate: Sift some cocoa powder on top of the cake, then add a few ladyfingers on top to decorate.

Serve: Cut into eight slices to serve.

Store: Covered in the fridge for up to two days.

Upside-down rhubarb cake

Serves 8

170g (¾ cup) salted butter, softened

170g (heaped ¾ cup) caster sugar

3 medium eggs

1 tsp vanilla bean paste

180g (1½ cups) self-raising flour

For the topping:

4 tbsp caster sugar

3 rhubarb stalks

60g (4 tbsp) salted butter, melted

To serve:

warm custard (page 182) or vanilla ice cream

Rhubarb is one of those underrated ingredients I get excited about when it comes back into season every year. This cake is sharp, sweet and always looks dramatic when you turn it out of the tin.

Prep: Preheat the oven to 190°C (375°F). Line the base of a 20cm (8in) springform cake tin.

Make the topping: Sprinkle the sugar all over the bottom of the lined tin. Slice the rhubarb stalks in half lengthways, then trim them down to size to fit in and completely cover the bottom of your tin. Put them on top of the sugar in an even layer, then pour over the melted butter.

Bake the topping: Bake in the preheated oven for 10 minutes to soften the rhubarb.

Make the cake: Meanwhile, using an electric mixer, beat the butter and sugar in a large mixing bowl for a few minutes, until pale and fluffy.

Beat in the eggs one at a time, beating until fully incorporated before adding the next egg. Stir in the vanilla.

Sift in the flour, then fold until there are no dry lumps left and the batter is smooth.

Bake the cake: Pour the batter over the baked rhubarb, then put the tin back in the oven and bake for 25–30 minutes, until the top of the cake is golden brown and a skewer inserted into the middle comes out clean.

Leave the cake to cool completely in the tin before inverting it onto a serving plate, then release the tin after it's been inverted.

To serve: Cut into eight slices. Serve with warm custard or a scoop of vanilla ice cream.

Store: Covered at room temperature for up to two days.

Victoria sponge

Serves 8

350g (1½ cups) salted butter, softened

350g (1¾ cups) caster sugar

6 medium eggs

1 tsp vanilla bean paste

350g (3 cups) self-raising flour

For the filling:

400g (1⅔ cups) double cream

350g (12oz) fresh strawberries, sliced

To decorate:

icing sugar, to dust

whole fresh strawberries

My mum said I couldn't write a baking book without a Victoria sponge in it. It's the first cake I properly baked by myself when I was just five years old. If that proves anything, it shows you can do it too!

Prep: Preheat the oven to 190°C (375°F). Line three deep 20cm (8in) cake tins with non-stick baking paper.

Make the cake: Using an electric mixer, beat the butter and sugar in a large mixing bowl for a few minutes, until pale and fluffy.

Add the eggs one at a time, beating until fully incorporated before adding the next egg. Stir in the vanilla.

Sift in the flour, then fold until there are no dry lumps left and the batter is smooth. Divide the batter evenly among the three lined tins.

Bake: Bake in the preheated oven for 15–20 minutes, until the cakes are golden on top and a skewer inserted into the middle of each one comes out clean.

Let the cakes cool in the tins for 10 minutes before turning out and transferring them to wire racks to cool completely.

Make the filling: Using an electric mixer, whisk the double cream in a medium mixing bowl until it reaches medium peaks.

Assemble: Put a dollop of whipped cream on the middle of a large serving plate, then put one cake layer on top of this (this helps stop the cake from moving around on the plate). Spread half of the whipped cream on top of this cake, then add half of the sliced strawberries.

Put the next cake layer on top of the strawberries and cream, then spread with the remaining whipped cream and add the rest of the sliced strawberries.

Add the last cake layer on top of the strawberries and cream.

Decorate: Using a small sieve, dust the top with icing sugar. Put a few whole fresh strawberries on top to decorate.

Serve: Cut into eight slices to serve.

Store: Covered in the fridge for up to two days.

Spiced Christmas cake

Serves 8–10

200g (¾ cup + 2 tbsp) salted butter, softened

200g (1 cup) caster sugar

3 medium eggs

150g (½ cup + 2 tbsp) buttermilk

zest and 3 tbsp juice from 1 large orange

zest of 1 lemon

400g (3⅓ cups) plain flour

2 tbsp ground nutmeg

1 tbsp ground ginger

1 tbsp ground cinnamon

1 tsp baking powder

1 tsp baking soda

For the dried fruit:

75g (½ cup) raisins

75g (½ cup) sultanas

20g (2 tbsp) mixed peel

2 tbsp plain flour

For the fondant:

2 tbsp apricot jam, melted

300g (11oz) marzipan

300g (11oz) ready-to-roll fondant icing

To decorate:

1 tbsp edible gold paint

To serve:

warm custard (page 182)

Does anyone have time for maturing and soaking their Christmas cake anymore? Maybe you do, but I definitely don't … or it's more likely that I forgot (oops!). This recipe is for the uncommitted or forgetful fruit cake lovers who still want a Christmas cake but without the alcohol (aka me).

Prep: Preheat the oven to 180°C (350°F). Line a 20cm (8in) springform cake tin with non-stick baking paper.

Prepare the dried fruit: Put the raisins, sultanas, mixed peel and flour in a small bowl, tossing until all the fruit is coated in flour. This prevents the fruit from sinking to the bottom of the cake.

Make the cake: Using an electric mixer, beat the butter and sugar in a large mixing bowl for a few minutes, until pale and fluffy.

Add the eggs, buttermilk, orange zest and juice and lemon zest and beat until combined.

Sift in the flour, spices, baking powder and baking soda, then fold until there are no dry lumps left and the batter is smooth. Fold in the flour-coated fruit. Pour the batter into the lined tin and smooth the top.

Bake: Bake in the preheated oven for 35–40 minutes, until a skewer inserted into the middle comes out clean.

Let the cake cool in the tin for 10 minutes before turning out and transferring to a wire rack.

For the fondant: Using a pastry brush, cover the top and sides of the cake with the melted apricot jam.

On a clean, dry work surface, roll out the marzipan until it's the size that will cover the top and sides of the cake. Using the rolling pin, lift the marzipan on top of the cake and smooth it out.

Roll out the fondant icing until it's the same size as the marzipan, then drape it on top, smoothing it over the top and sides.

Cut off any excess fondant and marzipan from around the base of the cake, then transfer it to a serving plate.

Decorate: Using a star cutter, lightly stamp stars into the fondant around the whole cake. Paint the pressed stars with edible gold paint.

Serve: My favourite way to serve this cake is with a generous helping of warm custard.

Store: In an airtight container at room temperature for up to five days.

Eton mess cupcakes

Makes 12

200g (¾ cup + 2 tbsp) salted butter, softened

200g (1 cup) caster sugar

3 medium eggs

1 tsp vanilla bean paste

200g (1⅔ cups) self-raising flour

For the meringue:

1 medium egg white

½ tsp cream of tartar

60g (¼ cup + 2 tsp) caster sugar

For the filling and topping:

200g (¾ cup + 4 tsp) double cream

12 tsp seedless strawberry jam, plus extra for drizzling

6 fresh strawberries, halved

Eton mess is chaos in dessert form, and in my opinion tastes better as a cupcake. If you're a messy baker, this recipe is perfect for you. The messier, the better!

Make the meringue: Preheat the oven to 150°C (300°F). Line a large baking tray with non-stick baking paper.

Scald a large metal bowl or the bowl of a stand mixer – do not use plastic! – with very hot water to remove any grease or residue, then dry it completely. Any grease or water would prevent the whites from whisking to peaks. Add the egg white and cream of tartar, then use a spotlessly clean electric mixer to whisk until soft peaks form.

Whisk in the sugar 1 tablespoon at a time, making sure the sugar is thoroughly incorporated before adding more. Whisk until very stiff peaks form – this could take 10 minutes or more.

Fill a piping bag with the meringue. Cut the tip off the piping bag and pipe small blobs of meringue onto the lined tray.

Bake the meringues in the preheated oven for about 20 minutes, until they are crisp when tapped and the centre of the meringues are completely dry when crushed.

Leave the meringues to cool, then store them in a dry place until ready to be used.

Make the cupcakes: Preheat the oven to 190°C (375°F). Line a 12-hole muffin tray with paper cases.

Using an electric mixer, beat the butter and sugar in a large mixing bowl for a few minutes, until pale and fluffy.

Add the eggs one at a time, beating until fully incorporated before adding the next egg. Stir in the vanilla.

Sift in the self-raising flour, then fold until there are no dry lumps left and the batter is smooth. Divide the batter evenly among the liners.

Bake in the preheated oven for 15–20 minutes, until the tops of the cupcakes are golden and the cake springs back when pressed.

Let the cupcakes cool fully on a wire rack.

Whip the cream: Using an electric mixer, whisk the cream in a medium mixing bowl until soft peaks form, being careful not to overmix the cream or it will curdle. Put the whipped cream in a piping bag with a star tip and set aside.

Decorate: Crush the meringues into rough crumbs.

Scoop out a little of the centre of each cupcake, then add 1 teaspoon of strawberry jam. Put the carved-out bit of the cupcake back on top of the jam centre.

Pipe large swirls of whipped cream on top of each filled cupcake. Drizzle each cupcake with a little more jam, then put a strawberry half on top. Finally, sprinkle some crushed meringue on top of each cupcake.

Store: Covered in the fridge for up to two days.

Triple chocolate chunk muffins

Makes 12

110g (½ cup) salted butter, melted

200g (1 cup) caster sugar

2 medium eggs

1 tsp vanilla bean paste

200g (¾ cup + 4 tsp) buttermilk

250g (2 cups) self-raising flour

70g (½ cup + 1 tbsp) cocoa powder

1 tsp baking powder

100g (3½oz) milk chocolate, cut into chunks

100g (3½oz) dark chocolate, cut into chunks

100g (3½oz) white chocolate, cut into chunks

What's better than one chocolate? Two chocolates. What's better than two chocolates? Three chocolates! These muffins are impressively rich and are exactly what I would always choose whenever I went to a bakery when I was younger.

Prep: Preheat the oven to 190°C (375°F). Line a 12-hole muffin tray with paper cases.

Make the muffins: Using an electric mixer, beat the butter and sugar together in a large mixing bowl for a few minutes, until pale and fluffy.

Add the eggs and vanilla and beat until combined, then stir in the buttermilk.

Sift in the flour, cocoa and baking powder, then fold until there are no dry lumps of flour or cocoa powder left and the batter is smooth.

Set aside some of the milk and dark chocolate chunks, then mix all the white chocolate chunks and the remaining milk and dark chocolate into the batter.

Scoop the batter into the paper cases, filling each one almost to the top of the case. This is what gives the muffins a lovely domed top. Sprinkle the reserved milk and dark chocolate chunks over the top of each case.

Bake: Bake in the preheated oven for 20–25 minutes, until a skewer inserted into the centre of a muffin comes out clean.

Let the muffins cool in the tray for a few minutes before moving them to a wire rack to cool completely.

Store: In an airtight container at room temperature for up to four days.

Caterpillar cakes

Makes 6 caterpillars

200g (¾ cup + 2 tbsp) salted butter, softened

200g (1 cup) caster sugar

3 medium eggs

2 tbsp whole milk

1 tsp vanilla bean paste

150g (1¼ cups) self-raising flour

30g (¼ cup) cocoa powder

For the ganache:

250g (9oz) dark chocolate, broken into pieces

500g (2 cups) double cream

To decorate:

white chocolate chips or mini marshmallows

food colouring (any colour)

6 flying saucer sweets

shoelace sweets

Smarties or M&Ms

sprinkles

These funky little caterpillar cakes are made purely to smile at. No caterpillar cake relies on your baking skill set, precision or ornate decorations. These cheerful cakes are easy to bake and are at home at every children's birthday party.

Prep: Preheat the oven to 190°C (375°F). Line two 24-hole mini cupcake trays with 48 paper liners.

Make the cupcakes: Using an electric mixer, beat the butter and sugar in a large mixing bowl for a few minutes, until pale and fluffy.

Add the eggs, milk and vanilla and beat until combined.

Sift in the flour and cocoa powder, then fold until there are no dry lumps left and the batter is smooth. Divide the batter evenly among the 48 cases.

Bake: Bake in the preheated oven for 10–12 minutes, until the cakes are springy and a skewer inserted into the middle comes out clean.

Remove the cupcakes from the trays and let them cool fully on wire racks. When the cupcakes are completely cool, peel off all the cases.

Make the ganache: Put the chocolate pieces in a medium heatproof bowl.

Pour the cream into a medium saucepan on a medium-high heat and simmer until it's just about to boil, stirring continuously so it doesn't catch on the bottom of the pan. As soon as it's about to boil, immediately take the pan off the heat and pour the hot cream over the chocolate. Let it sit for 10 minutes, then stir the cream and melted chocolate together until a smooth ganache is formed. Chill the ganache in the fridge for 30–45 minutes to let it firm up before use.

Assemble: Slice a small piece off the side of each mini cupcake so it has a flat surface when placed horizontally.

Put eight mini cupcakes on a serving plate, cut side down, lined up in a row. Using a small offset spatula, spread a thick layer of ganache over the tops and sides of the cupcakes. Spread it evenly, trying to keep some slight dimples between the cupcakes. Put a few white chocolate chips or mini marshmallows at the bottom of the cupcakes – these are the feet!

Put a small dab of food colouring on a toothpick, then use this to draw a face on the flying saucer sweet. Put it at the front of the cupcake caterpillar. Snip the shoelace sweets into strips 2.5cm (1in) long. Put two behind the flying saucer face – these are the caterpillar's antennas.

Scatter some Smarties or M&Ms and some sprinkles along the back of the caterpillar.

Repeat with the remaining cupcakes, ganache and sweets to make six caterpillars in total.

Store: Covered in the fridge for up to two days.

Funny face cupcakes

Makes 12

200g (¾ cup + 2 tbsp) salted butter, softened

200g (1 cup) caster sugar

3 medium eggs

1 tsp vanilla bean paste

200g (1⅔ cups) self-raising flour

For the icing:

150g (1¼ cups) icing sugar

2–3 tbsp cool water

To decorate:

24 Smarties or M&Ms

12 rhubarb and custard pips

6 chocolate buttons, cut in half

These cupcakes are very forgiving when it comes to decorating. They're not about perfection – they are joyful (and delicious!) even if their faces turn out a bit wonky.

Prep: Preheat the oven to 190°C (375°F). Line a 12-hole cupcake tin with paper cases.

Make the cupcakes: Using an electric mixer, beat the butter and sugar in a large mixing bowl for a few minutes, until pale and fluffy.

Add the eggs and vanilla, then beat until combined.

Sift in the flour, then fold until there are no dry lumps left and the batter is smooth. Divide the batter evenly among the 12 cupcake cases.

Bake: Bake in the preheated oven for 15–17 minutes, until the cupcakes are golden on top and spring back when pressed.

Let the cupcakes cool completely on a wire rack before icing.

Make the icing: Sift the icing sugar into a medium bowl. Whisk in just enough cool water to create a thick paste. Spread the thick icing on top of each cupcake.

Decorate: Press in two Smarties as eyes, one rhubarb and custard pip as a nose, and half a chocolate button as a mouth.

Store: In an airtight container at room temperature for up to three days.

TARTS, PASTRY & SWEET BREADS

Berry lovely jam tartlets

Makes 12

For the pastry:

250g (2 cups) plain flour, plus extra for dusting

30g (¼ cup) icing sugar, plus extra to decorate

125g (½ cup + 1 tbsp) salted butter, cold and cubed, plus extra for greasing

1 medium egg yolk

45g (3 tbsp) whole milk

For the filling:

12 heaped tbsp raspberry jam (or any other jam – see the intro)

For the egg wash:

1 medium egg, beaten

To decorate:

12 whole fresh raspberries

2 tbsp apricot jam

12 small fresh mint leaves

When I think of my childhood bakes, I think of jam tarts. I was obsessed with making pastry tarts after I received a rolling pin and a tart mould for Christmas one year. Jam was the simplest filling for a seven-year-old to put in a pastry base, but at the end of the day, jam and pastry will always taste lovely.

I use raspberry jam for these, but most other jams or even curds would work. Just don't use reduced-sugar jam, as it tends to burn. I also haven't had any luck with apple or grape jams, but trust me, I've tried!

Prep: Lightly grease a shallow 12-hole muffin tray.

Make the pastry: Put the flour and icing sugar in a medium bowl and stir to combine, then add the butter. Using your fingertips, rub everything together until a breadcrumb consistency is formed.

Make a small well in the centre of the bowl, then add the egg yolk and milk. Using your hands, bring everything together into a dough.

Alternatively, you could put the flour, icing sugar and butter in a food processor and blitz together until fine crumbs form, then add the egg yolk and milk and blitz again until it comes together into a dough.

Lightly dust a clean work surface with a little flour. Tip out the dough, then roll it out until it's about 5mm (¼in) thick (similar to the thickness of a euro coin).

Using a 7cm (2¾in) round cutter, stamp out 12 circles. Press these circles into the holes of the greased muffin tray, gently pressing the pastry over the base and up the sides, then prick each base once with a fork. Put the muffin tray in the freezer for 20 minutes to let the pastry bases firm up.

Bake: Preheat the oven to 180°C (350°F).

Bake in the preheated oven for 10 minutes. Remove the tray from the oven, then put 1 heaped tablespoon of raspberry jam in the centre of each base. Brush the pastry with egg wash. Put the tray back in the oven for 10 minutes, until the pastry is golden and slightly crisp.

Allow the tarts to cool in the tin. Do not touch the jam tarts until they are cool, as they are extremely hot! Tease them out of the tin with a teaspoon when they have fully cooled.

Decorate: Put a single raspberry on top of each tart.

Gently melt the apricot jam in a microwave-safe bowl in the microwave or in a small saucepan. Using a pastry brush, glaze the top of each tart, including the berry, with the melted jam. Dust over a little icing sugar.

Put a small mint leaf on top just before serving.

Store: In an airtight container in the fridge for up to three days, but without the mint leaf on top, as it will wilt.

Cherry Bakewell tart

Serves 10–12

For the pastry:

200g (1⅔ cups) plain flour, plus extra for dusting

50g (scant ½ cup) icing sugar

120g (½ cup + 2 tsp) salted butter, cold and cubed

1 medium egg yolk

For the frangipane:

125g (½ cup + 1 tbsp) salted butter, softened

125g (heaped ½ cup) caster sugar

125g (1¼ cups) ground almonds

50g (scant ½ cup) plain flour

2 medium eggs

1 tsp almond extract

For the egg wash:

1 medium egg, beaten

For the jam layer:

75g (⅓ cup) cherry jam

To finish:

a handful of fresh or canned cherries, stoned, halved and stems removed

a handful of flaked almonds

The cherry Bakewells I grew up with were coated in a heavy layer of icing and had a small glacé cherry half in the centre of the tart. These days, I enjoy the more traditional version of the tart, without the thick icing. Maybe that was a turning point in my maturing taste-buds ... or maybe it was just because of my constant lack of icing sugar in the pantry.

Make the pastry: Put the flour and icing sugar in a large bowl and stir to combine, then add the butter. Using your fingertips, rub everything together until a breadcrumb consistency is formed. Add the egg yolk and knead until it comes together into a shaggy dough. If the mixture is too dry, add a little cold water until a dough is formed.

Alternatively, you could put the flour, icing sugar and butter in a food processor and blitz together until fine crumbs form, then add the egg yolk and blitz again until it comes together into a dough.

Cover the bowl with cling film and chill in the fridge for 30 minutes.

Prep: Preheat the oven to 200°C (400°F).

Make the frangipane: Using an electric mixer, beat the butter, sugar, ground almonds, flour, eggs and almond extract in a large mixing bowl until combined into a paste consistency. Set aside.

Blind bake: Lightly dust a clean work surface with a little flour. Tip out the chilled pastry, then roll it out until it's a good bit larger than the base of a 25.5cm (10in) loose-bottomed fluted tart tin and about 5mm (¼in) thick. Lift the pastry into the tart tin and press it over the base and up the sides, pressing it into every groove. Cut off any excess pastry that's hanging over the sides.

Prick the bottom of the pastry all over with a fork, then cover it with a sheet of non-stick baking paper. Pour ceramic baking beans, dried beans or dried rice on top of the paper to weigh it down, then bake in the preheated oven for 10 minutes. Remove the tin from the oven, then remove the baking beans and paper and discard (be careful, baking beans can get VERY hot!). Brush the pastry with the egg wash, then put the tin back in the oven for a further 10 minutes, until the pastry is golden and crisp.

Finish: Spread the jam evenly over the base of the pastry shell. Add the frangipane on top of the jam and spread it across the whole tart in an even layer. Press the halved cherries into the frangipane, then scatter flaked almonds all over the tart.

Return to the oven and bake for a further 20–25 minutes, until the frangipane is set and the almonds are golden brown.

Allow to cool completely in the tin before removing the tart from the tin.

Serve: Cut into 10–12 slices to serve.

Store: Covered at room temperature for up to three days.

Lemon meringue pie

Serves 10–12

For the pastry:

200g (1⅔ cups) plain flour, plus extra for dusting

30g (¼ cup) icing sugar

110g (½ cup) salted butter, cold and cubed

1 medium egg yolk

For the lemon filling:

20g (2 tbsp) cornflour

zest and juice of 2 lemons

100g (½ cup) caster sugar

60g (4 tbsp) salted butter

4 medium egg yolks

For the meringue:

4 medium egg whites

250g (1¼ cups) caster sugar

½ tsp cream of tartar

Personally, I think lemon meringue pie is one of the most difficult desserts to make. Something about trying to set a lemon filling while keeping the meringue topping from collapsing is really hard to do. This recipe took the most amount of time to develop for this book and I couldn't be prouder of it.

Make the pastry: Put the flour and icing sugar in a large bowl and stir to combine, then add the butter. Using your fingertips, rub everything together until a breadcrumb consistency is formed. Add the egg yolk, then knead just until it comes together into a smooth dough. If the mixture is too dry, add a little cold water until a dough is formed.

Alternatively, you could put the flour, icing sugar and butter in a food processor and blitz together until fine crumbs form, then add the egg yolk and blitz again until it comes together into a dough.

Lightly flour a clean work surface, then roll out the pastry until it's about 5mm (¼in) thick and is large enough to cover the base and sides of a 25.5cm (10in) loose-bottomed fluted tart tin.

Being careful not to tear the pastry, lift it into the tin and press it firmly into the base and up the sides, working it into the grooves. Prick the base several times with a fork, then refrigerate for 30 minutes.

Blind bake: Preheat the oven to 190°C (375°F).

Put a sheet of non-stick baking paper on top of the chilled pastry base, then pour ceramic baking beans, dried beans or dried rice on top to weigh it down.

Bake in the preheated oven for 15 minutes, then carefully remove the baking beans and baking paper. Return to the oven and bake for another 5 minutes to brown the shell. Set aside on a wire rack to cool.

Make the filling: Put the cornflour and lemon juice in a large saucepan and whisk until smooth. Stir in the sugar, butter, egg yolks and lemon zest, then cook on a medium-low heat until the mixture begins to steam. Slowly raise the heat while stirring constantly until the mixture begins to boil. Pour the filling into the tart shell, then set aside.

Make the meringue: Using an electric mixer, whisk the egg whites, sugar and cream of tartar in a medium bowl for about 10 minutes, until stiff peaks form. Gently spread the meringue on top of the filled tart. Use a spoon or spatula to create peaks.

Bake: Bake the tart in the oven for 15–20 minutes, until the meringue has browned.

Allow to cool completely in the tin before removing the tart from the tin.

Serve: Cut into 10–12 slices to serve.

Store: Covered in the fridge for up to two days, but this tart is best eaten on the day it's made because the meringue might collapse.

Mini egg chocolate tartlets

Makes 12

For the pastry:

250g (2 cups) plain flour, plus extra for dusting

30g (¼ cup) icing sugar

125g (½ cup + 1 tbsp) salted butter, cold and cubed, plus extra for greasing

1 medium egg yolk

45g (3 tbsp) whole milk

For the egg wash:

1 medium egg, beaten

For the ganache filling:

100g (3½oz) dark chocolate, broken into small chunks

60g (4 tbsp) salted butter, diced into small pieces

100g (⅓ cup + 4 tsp) double cream

To decorate:

a small bag of mini chocolate eggs (12 whole eggs for the top and a few crushed for sprinkling)

My addiction to mini eggs every Easter is slightly embarrassing. In my efforts to cut down on the sheer number of mini eggs I eat, I make these tarts to get my chocolate fix.

Prep: Preheat the oven to 190°C (375°F). Grease a shallow 12-hole cupcake tray with butter.

Make the pastry: Put the flour and icing sugar in a large bowl and stir to combine, then add the butter. Using your fingertips, rub everything together until a breadcrumb consistency is formed.

Add the egg yolk and knead just until it comes together into a shaggy dough. If the mixture is too dry, add a little cold water until a dough is formed.

Lightly dust a clean work surface with a little flour, then roll out the pastry until it's about 5mm (¼in) thick (about the thickness of a euro coin). Using a 7cm (2¾in) round cutter, stamp out 12 circles. Press them into the base and up the sides of the greased holes of the cupcake tray. Brush the pastry with the egg wash, then prick the bottom of each tart once with a fork.

Bake: Bake the pastry cases in the preheated oven for 17–20 minutes, until crisp and golden and they come away from the tin easily. Using a teaspoon, gently prise the edges of the tart shells loose, then leave them to cool completely in the tin.

Make the ganache filling: Put the chocolate and butter in a medium heatproof bowl.

Pour the cream into a medium saucepan on a low heat, stirring constantly until it's hot enough to comfortably dip your finger in, but not boiling. Pour the hot cream over the chocolate and butter. Let it sit for 2 minutes, then stir together until a smooth ganache is formed.

Pour the chocolate ganache into a piping bag without a nozzle. Snip the tip off the bag, then pipe the ganache into the cooled tart shells until each one is full.

Decorate: Put a mini egg on top of each tart, then sprinkle over the crushed mini eggs. Chill the tarts in the fridge for a few hours, until the ganache is solid.

Store: In an airtight container in the fridge for up to two days.

Mince pies

For the pastry:

400g (3⅓ cups) plain flour, plus extra for dusting

100g (¾ cup) icing sugar

200g (¾ cup + 2 tbsp) salted butter, cold and cubed, plus extra for greasing

1 medium egg yolk

For the mincemeat filling:

100g (⅔ cup) raisins

100g (⅔ cup) sultanas

50g (4 tbsp) mixed peel

75g (⅓ cup) caster sugar

1 small Granny Smith apple, peeled, cored and finely chopped

zest and juice of ½ large orange

1 tbsp mixed spice

For the egg wash:

1 medium egg, beaten

To decorate:

icing sugar, to dust

To serve:

whipped cream

My mince pies are a bit famous among my relatives, so I make hundreds of them every Christmas to satisfy everyone's cravings. (And for my American readers who often ask me this question, no, mincemeat doesn't contain any meat.)

Make the mincemeat: Put all the mincemeat ingredients in a medium bowl and stir together. Cover the bowl, then put it in the fridge overnight to allow the fruit to absorb the orange juice.

Prep: Preheat the oven to 200°C (400°F). Grease a 12-hole cupcake tray with butter.

Make the pastry: Put the flour and icing sugar in a large bowl and stir to combine, then add the butter. Using your fingertips, rub everything together until a breadcrumb consistency is formed.

Add the egg and knead just until it comes together into a shaggy dough. If the mixture is too dry, add a little cold water until a dough is formed.

Lightly dust a clean work surface with a little flour, then roll out the pastry until it's about 5mm (¼in) thick (about the thickness of a euro coin). Using a 7cm (2¾in) circle cutter, stamp out 24 rounds. Press 12 of the rounds into the base and up the sides of the greased holes of the cupcake tray and prick the bases with a fork.

Put 1 heaped tablespoon of mincemeat in each pastry case, then put a pastry circle on top and press the edges together to seal. Brush with the egg wash, then cut a small cross on top of each pie to let the steam escape as they bake.

Bake: Bake in the preheated oven for 15–20 minutes, until the pastry is golden brown on top and crisp. Leave the mince pies in the tray and let them cool completely.

Decorate: Remove the cooled mince pies from the tray, then dust the tops with icing sugar.

Serve: Reheat the mince pies to serve them warm with a generous dollop of whipped cream.

Store: In an airtight container at room temperature for up to three days.

Deep-dish apple pie

Serves 10–12

For the pastry:

500g (4¼ cups) plain flour, plus extra for dusting

30g (2 tbsp) light brown sugar

225g (1 cup) salted butter, cold and cubed, plus extra for greasing

1 medium egg yolk

75g (⅓ cup) whole milk

For the filling:

2kg (approx. 4½lb) cooking apples, such as Bramley (approx. 8 large apples)

100g (½ cup) caster sugar

To finish:

1 medium egg, beaten

1–2 tbsp caster sugar

To serve:

vanilla ice cream or warm custard (page 182)

Every autumn, I get a glut of Bramley apples. I have far too many to bake a small tart with, hence this deep-dish version. I don't add any spices to my apple filling, as I like to let the apples do all the work and I enjoy their slight sourness against a custard or vanilla ice cream, but you can add cinnamon or nutmeg or more sugar.

Prep: Preheat the oven to 200°C (400°F). Grease a deep 25.5cm (10in) pie dish with butter.

Make the pastry: Put the flour and sugar in a large bowl and stir to combine, then add the butter. Using your fingertips, rub everything together until a breadcrumb consistency is formed.

Put the egg yolk and milk in a small jug and whisk together. Make a well in the middle of the dry ingredients, then pour in the milk mixture little by little, kneading just until a smooth dough is formed. If the mixture is too dry, add a little cold water until a dough is formed.

Divide the dough into two portions: one-third for the top and two-thirds for the crust. Put the smaller portion back in the bowl, cover with cling film and chill it in the fridge until needed.

Lightly dust a clean work surface and a rolling pin with a little flour. Roll out the larger portion of dough into a circle that's big enough to cover the base and sides of your deep pie dish.

Being careful not to tear the pastry, lift it into the dish and smooth it into the corners. Prick the base all over with a fork, then cut off any excess pastry that's hanging over the sides.

Bake: Bake the pastry in the preheated oven for 13–15 minutes, until it's a pale gold colour around the edges – the pastry base should not be fully cooked yet. Remove it from the oven and set aside on a wire rack.

Make the filling: Peel and core the apples, then cut them into slices about 5mm (¼in) thick. Pour in just enough water to cover the base of a saucepan, then add the apples and put the pan on a medium-high heat. Bring to a boil, then reduce the heat and simmer for 2–3 minutes. (Boiling helps to prevent the apples from shrinking after they get baked in the pie.)

Using a slotted spoon, scoop the softened apples out of the saucepan, making sure to leave any excess liquid behind (it would make the pastry soggy). Spread the apples evenly into the par-cooked pastry base, then scatter the sugar on top.

Assemble: Remove the remaining pastry from the fridge. Knead it for 30 seconds to warm it up. Put the pastry on your lightly floured work surface, then roll it out into a circle that's just large enough to cover the top of the dish. Gently drape the pastry over the top of the apple filling. Press the edges together to seal, then use a sharp knife to slice off any excess pastry hanging over the edges of the dish.

Cut a small cross in the centre of the pastry lid to let the steam escape. Brush the top all over with the beaten egg, then sprinkle generously with caster sugar.

Bake: Bake in the middle of the oven for 20-25 minutes, until deep golden on top.

Serve: Allow to cool slightly, then serve while it's still warm with a scoop of vanilla ice cream or warm custard.

Store: Covered at room temperature for up to three days.

Strawberry éclairs

For the choux pastry:
70g (⅓ cup) salted butter
160g (⅔ cup) water
150g (1¼ cups) plain flour
3 medium eggs, beaten
red food colouring

For the filling:
200g (¾ cup + 4 tsp) double cream
225g (8oz) fresh strawberries, halved

Éclairs are supposedly difficult to make – but not this recipe! I have simplified choux pastry as much as I can to make éclairs at home. I've gone with strawberries, but you can fill them with different fruits or even dip the top of the éclairs in melted chocolate.

Prep: Preheat the oven to 200°C (400°F). Line a large baking tray with non-stick baking paper.

Using a pencil, mark the baking paper with eight 15cm (6in)-long lines, leaving enough space in between the lines to let the éclairs spread and rise. Flip the paper over to prevent the pencil lines from transferring to the base of the pastry.

Make the choux pastry: Put the butter and water in a large saucepan and bring to a boil.

Sift the flour into a separate bowl. Add it to the butter and water as soon as they come to a boil, then immediately beat to a paste with a wooden spoon. Cook the paste for about 2 minutes, until it begins to clump together and leaves no residual pastry on the sides of the pan. Take the pan off the heat and transfer the dough to a mixing bowl.

Using an electric mixer, beat the pastry for at least 5 minutes, until it begins to cool down. Little by little, stream in the beaten egg while beating constantly.

Put a circle-shaped tip in a piping bag, then paint lines of red food colouring up the sides of the bag. Gently scoop the pastry into the bag, being careful not to ruin the painted stripes.

Using the lines you drew as a guide, pipe eight 15cm (6in) lines of choux pastry onto the paper. Keep them finger shaped.

Bake: Bake in the preheated oven for 15–20 minutes, until the pastry is golden and crisp on the outside.

Cut each éclair in half lengthways. Put them back on the tray, cut sides facing up. Bake for another 5 minutes to dry out the insides of the éclairs. Allow to cool completely before filling.

Make the filling: While the choux pastry cools, whisk the double cream in a medium mixing bowl until soft peaks form. Scoop the whipped cream into a piping bag with a small circle nozzle.

Assemble: Put the halved strawberries on the bottom half of each éclair, then pipe whipped cream in between the gaps. Put the top half of the éclair on top of the strawberries and cream and gently sandwich the two halves together.

Store: Covered in the fridge and eat them on the day they're made.

Custard slice

Makes 12

For the rough puff pastry:

300g (2½ cups) plain flour, plus extra for dusting

175g (¾ cup) salted butter, cold and cubed

50g (¼ cup) cool water

30g (2 tbsp) salted butter, softened

For the egg wash:

1 medium egg, beaten

For the custard:

150g (¾ cup) caster sugar

75g (½ cup) cornflour

3 medium egg yolks

1 tbsp vanilla bean paste

400g (1⅔ cups) whole milk

125g (½ cup + 1 tbsp) salted butter, cold and cubed

To finish:

300g (10½oz) white fondant icing

I love a good custard slice and there are so many different variations (they're also known as vanilla slice), both with and without icing. I've even seen ones with passion fruit. This is the most basic version, but the simplicity is what makes it so good.

Prep: Line two 18cm x 28cm (7in x 11in) baking tins with non-stick baking paper.

Make the rough puff pastry: Put the flour and 175g (¾ cup) cubed butter in a medium mixing bowl. Using your fingertips, rub the butter into the flour, but leave large chunks of butter that aren't fully incorporated.

Pour in the cool water and bring everything together into a ball. If it's too dry, add a little more water, 1 teaspoon at a time, just until it comes together.

Lightly dust a clean work surface with a little flour. Tip out the dough, then roll it into a small square. Wrap in cling film and pop it in the freezer for 20 minutes.

When you take the dough out of the freezer, lightly dust your work surface with a little flour again. Unwrap the dough, then roll it out into a 20cm x 25cm (8in x 10in) rectangle.

Spread half of the softened butter over the surface of the dough, then cut it in half. Put one half on top of the other half, with the buttered sides pressed together. Wrap in cling film and freeze for another 20 minutes.

Roll out the dough on the lightly floured work surface into a 20cm x 25cm (8in x 10in) rectangle again. Spread the rest of the softened butter over the surface of the rolled dough and cut it in half again. Once again, put one half on top of the other half, with the buttered sides pressed together. Wrap in cling film and freeze for a final 20 minutes.

Roll the dough out to a 35cm x 56cm (14in x 22in) rectangle, then cut it in half. Put each sheet of dough on a lined tray, then brush the surface of each one with egg wash.

Bake: Bake in the preheated oven for 12–15 minutes, until crisp and golden on top. Let the pastry cool completely on the trays, then gently transfer them to a wire rack.

Make the custard: Put the sugar, cornflour, egg yolks and vanilla in a medium heatproof bowl. Whisk until smooth.

Put the milk in a large saucepan on a medium heat and bring to a simmer – do not boil. Slowly pour a few tablespoons of the hot milk into the egg mixture, stirring constantly so you don't scramble the eggs. Keep popuring in the milk little by little while stirring until all the milk has been incorporated.

Add the custard back to the saucepan and set it on a medium-high heat, stirring continuously until it thickens. This could take a few minutes.

When it has thickened, bring the custard to a boil. Once it's bubbling, remove the saucepan from the heat entirely.

Add the cubed butter, stirring until it has fully melted into the custard. Leave the custard to cool completely before assembling the custard slice.

Assemble: Line an 18cm x 28cm (7in x 11in) baking tin with non-stick baking paper, letting the paper overhang the sides so that you can use it to lift the slab out of the tin at the end.

Put one sheet of puff pastry in the base of the lined tin. Pour all the custard over the top of the pastry. Put the second sheet of pastry on top of the custard layer and refrigerate for 3 hours, until the custard has set fully.

Put the white fondant icing in a microwave-safe bowl and heat for 30-second intervals until it has melted fully. (Be careful, hot fondant is dangerous!) Alternatively, put the fondant icing in a small saucepan on a medium-low heat with a tiny splash of water to prevent the fondant icing from catching. Heat until melted, stirring continuously.

Pour the melted fondant over the top pastry layer and spread it out evenly. Allow the fondant to cool and set in the fridge for at least 4 hours or overnight before slicing.

Serve: Use the baking paper to lift the slab out of the tin and onto a chopping board. Cut the custard slice into 12 rectangles to serve.

Store: In an airtight container in the fridge for up to two days.

Butterscotch buns

500g (4¼ cups) strong white flour, plus extra for dusting

50g (¼ cup) caster sugar

60g (4 tbsp) salted butter, cold and cubed

1 medium egg

1 x 7g sachet (2¼ tsp) of fast-action dried yeast

200g (¾ cup + 4 tsp) lukewarm water

For the butterscotch syrup:

80g (⅓ cup) salted butter, melted

80g (4 tbsp) golden syrup

30g (2 tbsp) light brown sugar

For the filling:

110g (½ cup) salted butter, softened

30g (2 tbsp) light brown sugar

To serve:

warm custard (page 182)

I vividly remember making a version of these buns in bakery school and sharing them with my family that evening after class. My brother was downright distraught the next morning when he found out I had given all the remaining buns away. If that doesn't prove how good these sticky buns are, I don't know what does!

Prep: Line an 18cm x 28cm (7in x 11in) or 23cm (9in) square baking tin with non-stick baking paper.

Make the butterscotch syrup: Put all the syrup ingredients in a saucepan on a medium heat and melt them together, then pour the syrup into the lined tin and spread it across the bottom. Set aside.

Make the dough: Put the flour, sugar, butter, egg, yeast and water in the bowl of a stand mixer fitted with the dough hook. Knead for 10 minutes, until the dough is smooth and elastic (or you can do this by hand).

Cover the bowl with a clean tea towel and allow the dough to rest in a warm, draught-free place for 1 hour, until it has doubled in size.

For the filling: Lightly dust a clean work surface with a little flour. Punch down the dough, then tip it out and roll into a 25.5cm x 30.5cm (10in x 12in) rectangle. Spread the 110g (½ cup) of softened butter evenly across the surface of the dough, then sprinkle over the brown sugar.

Shape the rolls: Starting with the long side that's furthest from you, roll the dough towards you into a cylinder. Slice the cylinder into 12 even pieces, then put them on top of the butterscotch syrup in the lined tin, swirl side up. (If one side of the swirls is less attractive than the other, make sure that side is facing up, as it will become the bottom when the buns are flipped out of the tin.)

Cover the tin with a clean tea towel and put it in a warm, draught-free place again to prove for 1 hour, until doubled in size.

Bake: Preheat the oven to 180°C (350°F).

Bake in the preheated oven for 35–40 minutes, until the buns are deep golden on top.

Allow the buns to cool in the tin for a few minutes before inverting them onto a serving plate so that the butterscotch glaze is on top.

Serve: Serve the buns while they're still warm, with warm custard.

Store: In an airtight container at room temperature for up to three days. Reheat when serving to melt the butterscotch syrup.

Chocolate babka

Makes 1 loaf

150g (½ cup + 2 tbsp) lukewarm water

75g (⅓ cup) caster sugar

2 medium eggs

1 x 7g sachet (2¼ tsp) fast-action dried yeast

1 tsp vanilla bean paste

450g (3¾ cups) strong white flour, plus extra for dusting

150g (⅔ cup) salted butter, cold and cubed

For the filling:

100g (3½oz) dark chocolate, broken into pieces

30g (2 tbsp) salted butter

50g (1¾oz) milk chocolate, broken into small chunks

For the egg wash:

1 medium egg, beaten

This was one of the first recipe videos I ever created back in 2023. The video has long since disappeared, but the recipe has been floating around in the back of my mind and I've finally put it down on paper.

Prep: Line a 900g (2lb) loaf tin with non-stick baking paper. Lightly dust a clean work surface with a little flour.

Make the filling: In a small microwave-safe bowl, melt the dark chocolate in the microwave in 30-second increments, stirring after each one. Add the butter and heat for another 20 seconds to melt the butter. Or you can put the chocolate and butter in a heatproof bowl set on top of a saucepan of gently simmering water, making sure the water doesn't touch the bottom of the bowl, and melt them that way. Stir to combine, then set aside.

Make the dough: Put the water, sugar, eggs, yeast and vanilla in a large jug and whisk to combine. Set aside.

Put the flour and butter in a large bowl. Using your fingertips, rub them together to form a breadcrumb consistency. Make a well in the middle, then slowly pour in the wet ingredients while stirring to incorporate them into a shaggy dough.

Turn the dough out onto the floured surface and knead for 10 minutes, until the dough is smooth and elastic. Or you could do all this in a stand mixer fitted with the dough hook attachment.

Dust your work surface with a little more flour, then roll out the dough until it's a roughly 30.5cm x 35.5cm (12in x 14in). Spread the filling across the entire surface of the dough, then scatter over the milk chocolate chunks. Starting with one of the longer sides, roll up the dough tightly.

Shape the dough: Using a sharp knife, cut the dough vertically down the centre into two long strands, but leaving them joined together at the top. Twist the dough strands over one another to form a tight twist. Tuck the two ends under the twist, then put the dough twist in the lined loaf tin.

Brush the top with the egg wash, then cover the top of the tin loosely with a clean tea towel and set aside in a warm, draught-free place for about 1½ hours, until it has doubled in size.

Bake: Preheat the oven to 180°C (350°F).

Brush the babka with another coat of egg wash, then bake in the preheated oven for 35–40 minutes, until it's a rich golden brown on top and a skewer inserted into the middle comes out clean (although a little melted chocolate clinging to the skewer is to be expected).

Leave to cool in the tin for a few minutes before turning out onto a wire rack to cool completely.

Serve: Cut into slices to serve.

Store: In an airtight container at room temperature for up to two days.

OTHER SWEET THINGS

Pistachio and strawberry roulade

Serves 8

4 medium egg whites

1 tsp cream of tartar

200g (1 cup) caster sugar

For dusting:

icing sugar

For the filling:

100g (⅓ cup + 1 tbsp) pistachio paste

200g (¾ cup + 4 tsp) double cream

100g (3½oz) fresh strawberries, sliced

To decorate:

2 tbsp pistachio paste

crushed pistachios

sliced fresh strawberries

Roulade is a dessert I'm eager to eat every time I see it. I didn't come up with the idea of combining pistachio and strawberries with meringue, but I am ever so grateful to whoever did.

Prep: Preheat the oven to 180°C (350°F). Line a Swiss roll tray with non-stick baking paper.

Make the meringue: Scald a large metal bowl or the bowl of a stand mixer – do not use plastic! – with very hot water to remove any grease or residue, then dry it completely. Any grease or water would prevent a meringue from forming.

Put the egg whites and cream of tartar in the bowl. Using a spotlessly clean electric mixer, whisk on a high speed until stiff peaks form. This could take 5 minutes or more.

While still whisking the stiff egg whites, slowly add the sugar a few tablespoons at a time until fully combined.

Spread the meringue on the baking paper on the lined tray in an even layer to create a neat rectangle.

Bake: Bake in the preheated oven for 18–20 minutes, until the meringue is slightly crisp on top. Remove it from the oven and immediately put a clean damp tea towel on top of it. This helps prevent cracking while cooling. Allow to cool completely.

Dust with icing sugar: When the roulade has completely cooled, dust a large sheet of non-stick baking paper with icing sugar. Turn the meringue out onto it, with the top surface face down against the paper.

Make the filling: Spread the pistachio paste across the surface of the cooked meringue.

Using an electric mixer, whisk the cream in a medium mixing bowl until it's nice and thick, being careful not to overmix or it will curdle. Reserve a little whipped cream for decoration, spread the rest all over the pistachio paste, then scatter over the sliced strawberries.

Assemble: Starting from the longest edge closest to you, use the baking paper to help you roll the filled roulade into a swirl. Slide the roulade from the paper onto a large serving dish.

Decorate: Melt the extra 2 tablespoons of pistachio paste in the microwave or in a small saucepan on a medium-low heat.

Dollop the top of the roulade with the reserved whipped cream and drizzle with the melted pistachio paste, then scatter over some crushed pistachios and sliced strawberries.

Store: This roulade is best eaten on the day it's made, but it can be kept covered in the fridge for up to two days.

Chocolate meringue nests

Makes 12

5 medium egg whites

1 tsp cream of tartar

150g (¾ cup) caster sugar

1 heaped tbsp cocoa powder

For the whipped cream:

250g (1 cup) double cream

2 tbsp caster sugar

1 tsp vanilla bean paste

For dusting:

30g (¼ cup) cocoa powder

Meringue nests are traditionally filled with cream and fruit, but my love for chocolate trumps that combo. If you want an easy-going yet impressive dessert, this is the one for you.

Prep: Preheat the oven to 160°C (325°F). Line two large baking trays with non-stick baking paper.

Make the meringue: Scald a large metal bowl or the bowl of a stand mixer – do not use plastic! – with very hot water to remove any grease or residue, then dry it completely. Any grease or water would prevent a meringue from forming.

Put the egg whites and cream of tartar in the bowl. Using a spotlessly clean electric mixer, whisk on a high speed until stiff peaks form. This could take 5 minutes or more.

While still whisking the stiff egg whites, slowly add the sugar a few tablespoons at a time until fully combined.

Sift the cocoa powder into the bowl, then gently swirl it through the meringue. Do not mix the cocoa through the meringue fully – you want to create a marbled effect.

Put the meringue into a piping bag with a large circle tip. Pipe 12 large, fist-sized blobs on the lined baking trays. Using a spoon, hollow out the centre of each blob to make a well for the whipped cream later.

Bake: Bake in the preheated oven for 45–50 minutes, until the meringues are crisp and very lightly browned. Leave the meringues to cool on the trays while you whip the cream.

Make the whipped cream: Using an electric mixer, whisk the double cream and caster sugar in a medium mixing bowl until medium peaks form. Stir through the vanilla until combined.

Assemble: Spoon large blobs of the whipped cream into the well of each meringue. Using a small sieve, heavily dust each meringue nest with cocoa powder.

Store: Covered in the fridge until ready to serve. Serve on the day it's made, as the meringue will degrade from the moisture in the cream.

Meringue wreath

330g (heaped 1½ cups) caster sugar

15g (1½ tbsp) cornflour

7 medium egg whites

1 tsp cream of tartar

To decorate:

500g (2 cups) double cream

150g (5¼oz) fresh strawberries, halved

100g (3½oz) fresh blackberries

75g (2½oz) dark chocolate, cut into small chunks

30g (¼ cup) pistachios, chopped

a few small fresh mint leaves

Perfection is the opposite of what you want for a good meringue wreath. Dollops of cream, large cracks in the meringue and unevenly sized chunks of fruit all make the meringue wreath what it's supposed to be: wonky but made with love.

Prep: Preheat the oven to 160°C (325°F). Line a large baking tray with non-stick baking paper.

Make the meringue: Stir the caster sugar and cornflour together in a medium mixing bowl and set aside.

Scald a large metal bowl or the bowl of a stand mixer – do not use plastic! – with very hot water to remove any grease or residue, then dry it completely. Any grease or water would prevent a meringue from forming properly.

Put the egg whites and cream of tartar in the bowl. Using a spotlessly clean electric mixer, whisk for 1–2 minutes, until foamy.

Whisk in the sugar and cornflour mixture 1 tablespoon at a time, whisking for 20 seconds between each addition, until the meringue has formed stiff peaks and all the sugar has been added.

Using a spoon, dollop the meringue into a wreath-like shape on the lined baking tray.

Bake: Bake in the preheated oven for 45–50 minutes, until the meringue is crisp on the outside and comes away from the baking paper when gently lifted. Let the meringue wreath cool completely on the tray before decorating.

Decorate: Carefully transfer the wreath to a large serving plate.

Using an electric mixer, whisk the cream in a large mixing bowl until it's nice and thick, being careful not to overmix the cream or it will curdle.

Spoon the whipped cream on top of the wreath in small heaps across the entire surface, then scatter over the strawberries, blackberries, dark chocolate and chopped pistachios. Finish with the mint leaves.

Store: Covered in the fridge until ready to serve. Serve on the day it's made, as the meringue will degrade from the moisture in the cream.

Berry trifle

Serves 8

200g (¾ cup + 2 tbsp) salted butter, softened

250g (1¼ cups) caster sugar

3 medium eggs

1 tsp vanilla paste

250g (2 cups) self-raising flour

For the jelly:

6 gelatine leaves

300g (1¼ cups) elderflower cordial (or any fruit juice)

200g (¾ cup + 4 tsp) water

150g (5¼oz) fresh raspberries (two-thirds mashed, one-third left whole)

50g (1¾oz) fresh strawberries

50g (1¾oz) fresh blueberries

For the custard:

75g (½ cup) cornflour

400g (1⅔ cups) whole milk

100g (½ cup) caster sugar

20g (4 tsp) salted butter

3 medium egg yolks

1 tsp vanilla bean paste

For the whipped cream:

250g (1 cup) double cream

To decorate:

fresh strawberries, blueberries and raspberries

fresh mint leaves

Trifle is a firm favourite in my family, so when I was given a crystal trifle bowl that had been passed down from my great-grandma, I had to create a trifle that lived up to hers! But this recipe can be as easy or as difficult as you want it to be – there's nothing wrong with a packet of jelly or store-bought custard.

Prep: Preheat the oven to 190°C (375°F). Line an 18cm x 28cm (7in x 11in) or 23cm (9in) square baking tin with non-stick baking paper.

Make the cake: Using an electric mixer, beat the butter and sugar in a medium mixing bowl for a few minutes, until pale and fluffy. Add the eggs and vanilla and beat until combined.

Sift in the flour, then fold until there are no dry lumps left and the batter is smooth. Pour the batter into the lined tin, spreading it evenly into the corners.

Bake: Bake in the preheated oven for 20–25 minutes, until golden brown on top and a skewer inserted into the middle comes out clean.

Let the cake cool completely in the tin, then cut it into 2.5cm (1in) chunks. Put the cake chunks in a trifle dish.

Make the jelly: Put the gelatine leaves in a small bowl of water and allow to soften for a few minutes.

Heat the elderflower cordial and water in a medium saucepan on a medium-high heat until it's gently simmering. Take the pan off the heat and allow to cool slightly, then take the gelatine leaves out of the water and stir them into the warm cordial along with the mashed raspberries.

When it's cool to the touch but still liquid, pour the jelly on top of the cake chunks in the trifle dish. Scatter the strawberries, blueberries and whole raspberries evenly across the top of the jelly. Put the dish in the fridge for 2–3 hours, until the jelly has stiffly set.

Make the custard: Put the cornflour in a small bowl with a small splash of the milk, then whisk together until smooth.

Put the milk, sugar, butter, egg yolks, vanilla and cornflour mixture in a large saucepan on a medium-high heat and whisk together, then stir constantly until the custard thickens. When the custard is very thick – almost gloopy – remove the pan from the heat. Allow the custard to cool before assembling the trifle.

Whip the cream: Using an electric mixer, whisk the cream in a medium mixing bowl until it's nice and thick, being careful not to overmix or it will curdle.

Assemble: Spoon the custard over the jelly, then spread the whipped cream on top of the custard. Scatter over some fresh berries and mint leaves to decorate.

Store: Covered in the fridge for up to two days.

White chocolate and orange possets

Makes 6

4 large oranges

300g (1¼ cups) double cream

300g (10½oz) white chocolate, broken into chunks

These little possets always get curious looks at parties until you explain what they are. These single-serve desserts set in the fridge while you get on with everything else you're cooking, but when they're served, you will look like the most put-together person. Or you can do what I do and make them all for yourself and eat them over the course of a couple days. Who says you need to impress people?

Prepare the oranges: First zest one of the oranges and set that aside before cutting all the oranges in half and juicing them. Remove any of the remaining internal structure in six of the best-looking orange halves, down to the pith.

Put the six orange halves in a muffin tray for stability to make it easier to pour in the posset mixture later. Set aside.

Make the posset: Pour the cream into a medium saucepan on a medium-high heat and simmer until it's just about to boil, stirring continuously so it doesn't catch on the bottom of the pan. As soon as it's about to boil, take the pan off the heat and add the chocolate. Let it sit for 10 minutes, then stir the cream and chocolate together until melted and smooth. Add 3 tablespoons of orange juice and a pinch of the orange zest (you can just drink the rest of the juice – baker's treat!).

Pour the chocolate and cream mixture into the orange halves, going right up to the top. Put the muffin tray holding the oranges in the fridge for 2–3 hours to allow the possets to set.

Serve: Sprinkle the rest of the orange zest on top of the possets to decorate. The possets are best served straight from the fridge.

Store: Covered in the fridge for up to two days, but only sprinkle the orange zest on top just before serving.

Fondant fancies

Makes 16

200g (¾ cup + 2 tbsp) salted
butter, softened

250g (1¼ cups) caster sugar

3 medium eggs

1 tsp vanilla bean paste

250g (2 cups) self-raising flour

For the buttercream:

200g (1⅔ cups) icing sugar

150g (⅔ cup) salted butter,
softened

For the icing:

1kg (2¼lb) ready-to-roll
fondant icing

food colouring (any colour)

icing sugar, for dusting

To decorate:

100g (3½oz) dark chocolate

Fondant fancies look impressive, but I want to demystify them. Once you break them down, they're surprisingly achievable to make at home. I chose the simple route with roll-out fondant instead of pouring. Even with all my baking training and experience, you will never see me pouring icing!

Prep: Preheat the oven to 200°C (400°F). Line an 18cm x 28cm (7in x 11in) baking tin with non-stick baking paper, letting the paper overhang the sides so that you can use it to lift the cake out of the tin at the end.

Make the cake: Using an electric mixer, beat the butter and sugar in a large mixing bowl for a few minutes, until pale and fluffy.

Add the eggs and vanilla and beat until combined.

Sift in the flour, then fold until there are no dry lumps left and the batter is smooth. Pour the batter into the lined tin.

Bake: Bake in the preheated oven for 20–25 minutes, until golden on top and a skewer inserted into the middle comes out clean.

Let the cake cool completely in the tin. When fully cooled, use the paper to lift the cake out of the tin, then cut it into 16 small squares.

Make the buttercream: Sift the icing sugar into a medium mixing bowl, then add the butter. Using an electric mixer, beat until very pale and smooth – this can take up to 10 minutes. If the mixture is looking quite dry, add 1 tablespoon of cold water and continue to beat until smooth.

Put the buttercream in a piping bag fitted with a 1cm (½in) round circle tip. Set aside.

Add the fondant: Put the fondant on a clean, dry work surface. Add a few drops of food colouring, then knead it in until it's evenly mixed throughout with no streaks.

Sprinkle some icing sugar on the work surface. Roll out the fondant on the dusted work surface until it's a large rectangle about 50.5cm x 58.5cm (20in x 23in).

Using a sharp a knife, cut the fondant into 16 squares, making sure they are all large enough to completely cover each cake square. Set aside.

Make the chocolate stripes: In a small microwave-safe bowl, melt the dark chocolate in the microwave in 30-second increments, stirring after each one. Or you can put the chocolate in a heatproof bowl set on top of a saucepan of gently simmering water, making sure the water doesn't touch the bottom of the bowl, and melt it that way.

Let the chocolate cool for several minutes before transferring it to a small piping bag with no tip.

Assemble: On top of every cake square, pipe a small blob of buttercream icing directly in the centre.

Put a square of fondant on top of each cake square, smoothing it over the sides but being careful not to squish the blob of icing so that it keeps its domed shape on top. Cut away any excess fondant from the edges of each square.

Snip the top off the piping bag of melted chocolate, then drizzle lines over the top of each fondant fancy. Allow the chocolate to harden and set before serving.

Store: In an airtight container at room temperature for up to three days.

Orange and white chocolate madeleines

Makes 12

For the tin:

15g (1 tbsp) salted butter, melted

a little plain flour, for dusting

For the madeleines:

110g (½ cup) salted butter, melted

75g (⅓ cup) caster sugar

2 medium eggs

zest of 1 large orange

120g (1 cup) plain flour

1 tsp baking powder

For the orange syrup:

juice of 1 large orange

cold water

75g (⅓ cup) caster sugar

For the white chocolate topping:

200g (7oz) white chocolate, chopped

Madeleines feel like a small luxury, but are so simple to make. The orange adds a gentle citrus flavour that makes them perfect with a cup of tea. When you want to feel fancy, these are the thing to bake.

Prep: Preheat the oven to 190°C (375°F).

Use the 15g (1 tablespoon) of melted butter to grease the madeleine tin. Use a pastry brush and make sure you get into every nook and cranny. Dust the tin lightly all over with flour, then tap out the excess. Chill the prepared tin in the fridge until needed.

Make the madeleines: Mix the 110g (½ cup) melted butter and sugar together in a mixing bowl, then beat in the eggs until fully incorporated. Save a little orange zest for decoration, then add the rest to the butter, sugar and egg.

Sift in the flour and baking powder, then fold until there are no dry lumps left and the batter is smooth.

Put 1 tablespoon of batter into each mould in the prepared tin, then give the tin a little shake to flatten the batter in the moulds.

Bake: Bake in the preheated oven for 10–12 minutes, until the madeleines are golden brown and have risen in the centres. Let the madeleines cool in the tin for 15 minutes to prevent any cracking when removing them. When the 15 minutes are up, gently tease them out of the moulds with a teaspoon. Put them on a wire rack to cool completely.

Make the orange syrup: Measure your orange juice to see how much you have, then put it in a small saucepan with the same amount of cold water (in other words, you want a 1:1 ratio of orange juice to water). Add the sugar, then bring to a boil, stirring constantly. As soon as it boils, take the pan off the heat and allow to cool completely.

Dip the flat bottom of each madeleine into the cooled orange syrup, then put them back on the wire rack to dry.

Melt the white chocolate: In a small microwave-safe bowl, melt the white chocolate in the microwave in 30-second increments, stirring after each one. Or you can put the chocolate in a heatproof bowl set on top of a saucepan of gently simmering water, making sure the water doesn't touch the bottom of the bowl, and melt it that way.

Dip the top of each madeleine into the melted white chocolate, then sprinkle a small pinch of the reserved orange zest on top. Put the madeleines back on the wire rack and allow the chocolate to set for about 20 minutes before eating.

Store: In an airtight container at room temperature for up to a day, but these are best eaten on the day they're made.

Plum crumble

Serves 8

For the plum base:

12 large plums, stoned and cut into quarters

125g (heaped ½ cup) caster sugar

1 tsp ground cinnamon

1 tsp ground nutmeg

For the crumble:

500g (4¼ cups) plain flour

225g (1 cup) salted butter, cold and cubed

150g (heaped ¾ cup) light brown sugar

To serve:

warm custard (page 182) or vanilla ice cream

You really can't go wrong with a crumble. I like to bake this plum crumble in a big batch, freeze it, then break off a chunk and reheat it in the microwave with custard whenever I need some warmth. But this recipe is less about my guilty pleasures and more about how fantastically easy it is to make a crumble.

Prep: Preheat the oven to 190°C (375°F).

Make the plum base: Grab a large saucepan and pour in just enough water to cover the base of the pan. Add the plums, then bring to a boil on a high heat. Reduce the heat and cook for 5–8 minutes, until the plums have softened slightly. Remove from the heat and strain off and discard any liquid in the pan.

Stir in the sugar, cinnamon and nutmeg until the plums are coated. Transfer the plums to a large roasting dish (about 28cm x 40cm / 11in x 16in), making sure they are spread out evenly across the base.

Make the crumble: Put the flour, butter and brown sugar in a large bowl. Using your fingertips, rub in the butter until large clumps form.

Assemble: Sprinkle the crumble over the plums in the roasting dish. Keep the crumble loose – don't press it down – so it cooks evenly.

Bake: Bake in the preheated oven for 30–35 minutes, until the plums have broken down and the crumble topping is a deep golden brown.

Serve: Serve the crumble while it's still warm, with warm custard or a scoop of vanilla ice cream.

Store: Covered in the fridge for up to two days or in the freezer for up to a month.

Chocolate strawberry fudge

Makes 24 pieces

450g (1lb) dark chocolate, broken into chunks

1 x 397g (14oz) can of condensed milk

20g (1½ cups) freeze-dried strawberries

Chocolate-covered strawberries are a simple treat to make if you want to show your love for someone, but I'd much rather have fudge. Chocolate fudge with strawberries? Now that's true love.

Prep: Line an 18cm x 28cm (7in x 11in) baking tin with non-stick baking paper.

Make the fudge: Melt the chocolate and condensed milk together in a medium saucepan on a medium-high heat, stirring constantly. When the chocolate has melted, stir in most of the freeze-dried strawberries.

Spread the fudge mixture into the lined tin and smooth the top, then press the remaining freeze-dried strawberries on top. Chill the fudge in the fridge for 1 hour, until set fully, then cut it into 24 small squares.

Store: In an airtight container in the fridge for up to three days.

Ani's cheesy treats

Makes 12

150g (2 cups) rolled oats

150g (1 cup) whole wheat flour

100g (heaped ⅓ cup) plain, unsweetened Greek yogurt

35g (⅓ cup) grated Cheddar cheese

1 small carrot, grated

1 medium egg, beaten

Anyone who follows me on social media knows Ani, my beloved Lhasa Apso. She is always by my side (and under my feet when I'm baking!), so I couldn't resist sneaking in an extra recipe for her. I hope your dog loves these treats as much as she does.

Prep: Preheat the oven to 180°C (350°F). Line a large baking tray with non-stick baking paper.

Make the dough: Put all the ingredients in a large bowl. Using your hands, mash everything together until a smooth-ish dough forms.

Tip the dough out onto a clean work surface, then roll it out until it's about 1cm (½in) thick. Using a dog bone cookie cutter (or any shape), stamp into 12 biscuits (or as many as you can get). Transfer to the lined baking tray.

Bake: Bake in the preheated oven for 25–30 minutes, until set firm.

Serve: Allow the treats to cool completely on a wire rack before letting your dog enjoy them.

Store: In an airtight container for up to four days.

Index

Thank you

To my supporters online, the digital world felt like a strange place when I first started posting, and honestly, I was still finding my footing too. From sharing my horse-box journey at 18 to the skits and the baking tutorials, you've been there for it all. Your kindness and constant support turned a small corner of the internet into my dream job. I could thank you forever, but instead, I made this book for each and every one of you, baker or not.

To my parents, thank you for always letting me chase what I wanted, even when my path wasn't clear. Mum, thank you for giving me space in the kitchen and trusting me to turn it into something I loved. You taught me my first bake and I will be eternally grateful for that. Dad, thank you for standing beside me with the horse-box, especially on the days I wanted to give up, and for the 5am mornings towing it to a location. The constant support from you both has shaped who I am. You are not only incredible parents, but truly wonderful people, and I hope to carry a part of you both with me into everything I become.

To my brother, Thomas, I know you enjoy only a select few of my cakes, but thank you for always showing up in my videos, never telling me when I'm being a bit too cringeworthy and for putting up with me filming while you're just trying to work. You're a legend.

To my gorgeous friend Roisin, thank you for making almost every cookie photographed in this book. While I wrote the recipes, your magic hands made them ten times better. You are a ray of sunshine, and the very best thing to come out of my time at bakery school was our friendship.

To Mihai, thank you for being my rock and my best friend throughout my teenage years, and still now, and always. I'm endlessly grateful for your guidance and honest judgement in every opportunity I take, and for being there to witness milestones like the day I was offered this book opportunity. Most of all, thank you for sharing every bit of the excitement along the way. Even on the bad days, you've been my light. Love you!

To my family and friends, I'm sorry for keeping this book such a big secret! There were so many moments I wanted to spill the beans. You guys have kept me going through thick and thin, and even if you weren't aware of it, this book only happened because I knew I had support from all of you. And to my Irish granny Margarita, growing up with your cupcakes and apple tarts was the best part of my childhood.

And of course, thank you to the amazing team of women who worked on this book alongside me.

To Kristin, my publisher, from the first time we met at Jolene and Lily Mae Cox's book launch to now having my own book with Nine Bean Rows, you have guided me through every step with a level of compassion and wisdom that is truly rare. You made this book possible, and I will be forever grateful for the opportunity you've given me. Also, you're incredible, and I probably haven't said that enough!

Charlotte, your food styling skills are unmatched. Every bake in this book came to life through your magic touch (I'm still incredibly jealous of your fork collection).

Jo, you and your camera are unstoppable. The photos you captured of my bakes are nothing short of astonishing. Working in a small corner of my kitchen, you somehow made every bake look a million times better than I ever imagined.

Jane, who designed this entire book from the front cover to the very last page, I'm so grateful for your patience in letting me be a little picky when I needed to be. You are an incredible designer.

Emma M., thank you for putting all the meetings together, for explaining everything that goes into the publicity for a book that I never would have realised, and of course for handing me amazing opportunities for this book. You are a fabulous publicist.

Donna, my make-up artist for the cover, your talent is unreal. You made me feel so confident and beautiful during the shoot, and I'm so thankful for that.

Emma D., my hair stylist for the cover, thank you for truly listening and embracing my slightly wacky hair. You kept me looking effortlessly stylish, and I couldn't have asked for better.

And last but not least, to Ani the dog, thank you for sitting still (occasionally) for photos and for weaving between our feet for the entire book shoot. Recipe number 81 is for you.

Nine Bean Rows

23 Mountjoy Square

Dublin, D01 E0F8

Ireland

@ninebeanrows

ninebeanrowsbooks.com

First published 2026

001

Text copyright © Alice Kelly, 2026

Photography copyright © Jo Murphy, 2026

ISBN: 978-1-0684050-5-1

Editor: Kristin Jensen

Proofreader: Susan Low

Designer: Jane Matthews

Photographer: Jo Murphy

Food stylist: Charlotte O'Connell

Printed by L&C Printing Group, Poland

This product is made of material from well-managed, FSC®-certified forests

and other controlled sources.

All rights reserved.

No part of this publication may be copied, reproduced or transmitted in any

form or by any means without written permission of the publishers.

A CIP catalogue record for this book is available from the British Library.

For EU product safety concerns, contact info@ninebeanrowsbooks.com.